GEOFF
BRADFORD

GEOFF BRADFORD

BRISTOL ROVERS LEGEND

IAN HADDRELL & MIKE JAY

The
History
Press

First published 2012

The History Press
The Mill, Brimscombe Port
Stroud, Gloucestershire, GL5 2QG
www.thehistorypress.co.uk

British Library Cataloguing in Publication Data.
A catalogue record for this book is available from the British
Library.

ISBN 978 0 7524 6528 9

Typesetting and origination by The History Press
Printed in Great Britain

CONTENTS

ACKNOWLEDGEMENTS

The greatest thanks of all are, of course, due to the authors' wives, Julie and Diane, without whose love, care and support this book would never have been possible. No book containing this degree of information could be a feasible proposition without recourse to considerable help from a number of sources. Stephen Byrne, a fellow Rovers historian, has given tirelessly and unstintingly of his time and has unearthed many snippets of invaluable information during his long hours in the newspaper vaults at Bristol Central Library. Despite a move with his family to work in Kenya three years ago he has continued to contribute greatly. We are as indebted to him for his input and proof reading, as we are to Dennis Payter, the former *Bristol Evening Post* journalist, for loaning us the many items he obtained from the Bradford family archive. We thank Lynn and Nichola, Geoff's daughters, for their willingness to share otherwise inaccessible memorabilia and information on their father's life, as well as Geoff's sister Joan and nephew Paul for their help. Bristol Rovers programme editor Keith Brookman kindly allowed access to both the many images collected over the past fifteen years and to the Bristol Rovers records in his possession. The late Alan Lacock was always an excellent source of statistical details relating to Rovers players.

Of the many people whose help has contributed to the production of this volume, we are also indebted, in no particular order but with very grateful thanks in every case, to former team-mates of Geoff, namely: Bill Roost, Josser Watling, Harold Jarman, Ray Mabbutt, Bernard Hall, Joe Davis, the late Peter Hooper, Howard Radford and the late Alfie Biggs. Of course many generations of supporters will have seen Geoff play and have a view on Geoff's contribution over the fifteen years he was at Bristol Rovers. These include former *Bristol Evening Post* journalist Eddie Giles, Peter Missen, Mo Bell, and Bernard Brain. We also would like to thank Phil Turner, Mike Heal, George Belcher and Ray Hazzard for their contributions. Thank you to you all for your time, energy and encouragement. While every effort has been made to ensure that the details included in this book are as accurate as possible, errors are an inevitability in a work of this magnitude and the authors apologise for these in advance. We are also keen to point out that any opinions stated are our own views, reflecting on the statistics to hand, and not necessarily those of Bristol Rovers Football Club.

Research for this book has necessitated a thorough investigation of local newspapers, primarily the *Bristol Evening World*, *Western Daily Press* and *Bristol Evening Post*. The authors have visited a wide range of libraries to consult all manner of newspapers and journals and our thanks are due to the staff at each of these. Other books which have provided valuable information and may be of further interest to the reader include:

Atyeo: The Hero Next Door, Tom Hopegood & John Hudson, Redcliffe Press, 2005

Bristol Rovers: The Definitive History 1883–2003, Stephen Byrne & Mike Jay, Tempus, 2003

Bristol Rovers Miscellany: Rovers Trivia, History, Facts and Stats, Stephen Byrne, Pitch, 2010

Bristol Rovers On This Day: History, facts and figures from every day of the year, Stephen Byrne, Pitch, 2009

Inspection of Bristol Rovers Football Club Limited, Board of Trade, HMSO, 1951

Pirates in Profile: A Who's Who of Bristol Rovers Players 1920–1994, Stephen Byrne & Mike Jay, Potton, Baber & Murray, 1994

The Bert Tann Era, Edward Giles, Desert Island Football Histories, 2007

FOREWORD

I have three main memories of Geoff Bradford, Bristol Rovers' record scorer with a hunger for hat-tricks. Above all, the courageous and indefatigable manner in which he battled back from those two truly horrendous injuries. Next, the strength of character he also showed when called a blackleg and threatened with being ostracised by team-mates against whom he stood alone in refusing to vote for a strike aimed at abolishing the maximum wage. He foresaw drawbacks that have since become all too apparent, with power concentrated into an elite band of the wealthier clubs.

Thirdly, there was the unfairness of Bradford's exclusion from the England team after scoring in the victory on his international debut. Strong as the competition for places was, notably from a young upstart named Johnny Haynes, it clearly counted against the Rovers sharpshooter that he was outside the First Division with a so-called unfashionable club. Which raises the intriguing question of how he would have fared if he had played regularly at that level instead of loyally remaining a one-club man? I am with those who fancy that the goals would still have flowed.

Eddie Giles

Eddie Giles started his journalistic career with the *Derby Evening Telegraph* in 1944 where he spent twelve years – less three away while on National Service in the RAF. Moving to Bristol in 1956, Giles became deputy sports editor of the *Bristol Evening Post* and later chief sports sub-editor until 1970 when he joined the *Daily Telegraph,* first in Manchester and then in London. For the last eight years until his retirement in 1993 he was that newspaper's northern sports editor. He has written many football books on Derby County, Bristol City and Bristol Rovers plus one on perhaps England's finest international centre forward, Tommy Lawton. He is a life member of the National Union of Journalists.

OUR LOYAL ROVER

Posted to all kinds of stations,
GEOFF was never known to fail,
And, for sticky situations,
Always ready on the nail!

Geoff and manager Bert Tann were featured in a 1950s newspaper cartoon depicted at the famous Nails in Corn Street, Bristol.

1

EARLY FAMILY LIFE

On 18 July 1927 Mr Albert and Mrs Emily Bradford's (née Lambourne) fourth child, Geoffrey Reginald William, was born at 2 Belle Vue Cottages, Clifton Wood, a cul-de-sac of terraced houses, a continuation of Belle Vue Crescent located on the slopes behind the public baths on Jacobs Wells Road. One of the oldest and most affluent areas of Bristol situated to the west of the city centre, Clifton was at one time a separate settlement but became attached to Bristol by continuous development during the Georgian period and was formally incorporated into the city in the 1830s. Grand houses that required many servants were built in the area, and while a good number were detached or semi-detached properties, the bulk were built as terraces, many with three or more floors. Little did Albert, a police constable with Bristol Constabulary's 'E' Divison, and Emily appreciate at the time that their newborn son, Geoff, as he would be known, was destined to be Bristol Rovers' most famous footballer.

A year after Geoff's birth, the Bradford family vacated Belle Vue Cottages and moved to 36 Holly Grove, Hillfields, a north-eastern suburb of Bristol adjacent to the Soundwell and Staple Hill districts of the city. Geoff and his siblings, Donald, Joan and Mabel (known as Bett), attended Soundwell Primary School, located in Church Road opposite Soundwell's football ground, half a mile from the family home.

From about the age of 6 Geoff showed a keen interest in football and as most young boys do he enjoyed joining in kick-abouts with his friends and older brother. Despite his lack of size Geoff had a real passion for the game and tried to improve at every opportunity – if Geoff didn't have a ball to play with he would resort to kicking a tin can instead. On numerous occasions his football was kicked into the garden of Mrs Jones, a neighbour who lived opposite the Bradford family. She constantly threatened that she would keep the young lad's ball if it came over again – but she never did. On one occasion after Geoff's mother had bought him a new pair of shoes and he was outside kicking a ball while wearing them, she told him to stop playing and come into the house or his new footwear would be scuffed and worn out in no time. But Geoff, in common with all young boys, took no notice. Despite his obvious enthusiasm for the game, his talent (if it had manifested itself at the time) was not recognised. His junior school games master once told a disappointed Geoff to forget about football because he considered him to be too small for the game. This acted as a challenge to Geoff to prove the teacher wrong and frequently he would walk from his house with his

The Bradford family photographed at Laurence Studios in Bristol, c. 1931. Standing: Donald (born 1920). Seated, left to right: Joan (born 1923), Geoff (born 1927), Mabel (born 1924).

Geoff and his sister Joan, with their dog Jim, standing outside their home in Lincombe Avenue, Downend, c. 1937. Geoff's mother used to send Jim to school to bring Geoff home, which he dutifully did!

Staple Hill Torchbearers Youth Football Club played in the Kingswood & District Youth Association League. Geoff is pictured sixth from the right wearing a snake belt to keep his shorts up.

football to the common land which led to Soundwell Football Club to play and practice the game he loved.

On one occasion the family was getting ready in their best clothes to visit Laurence Studios, the photographers in the centre of Bristol, to have a family portrait taken. Geoff was dressed and ready wearing his new teddy bear coat, and when his mother popped into another room to collect something she asked his sister, Bett, to keep her eye on him. Regrettably, she neglected to do this and the four-year-old Geoff made his escape into the street where he managed to fall into a muddy puddle, ruining the new coat. Fortunately a young friend of the family, Nellie Johnson, came to the rescue. She was studying music and dance and having a number of costumes was able to lend Emily an outfit for Geoff to wear, and so he ended up visiting the photographers in a blouse and satin trousers. 'He was always getting into trouble,' remembered his sister Joan, 'with kicking things and wearing his shoes out. From morning 'til night it was football. Football was his life and he gave it all he had. Brother Don was always playing war with him, as he was small and always getting in Don's way, and he would complain to Mum, but when she told Geoff off it went in one ear and out the other. Football was his life and he lived it.'

In about 1936, when Albert Bradford left his wife Emily and their four children, she moved from Hillfields initially to the Downend area, followed by a move to the Frenchay district on the outskirts of Bristol. In order to support the family, Emily ran a tea room serving drinks, sandwiches, cakes and cream teas to order. During the Second World War meals were cooked for the troops stationed on Frenchay Common, who used to walk down to the tea room through the woods for a good meal that was cooked on a large range and an electric cooker.

Geoff's sister Joan recalls two troops, Frank and Tom, who used to walk down to the tea room to buy food. Frank had a wonderful singing voice and on hearing him approaching singing, she would shout out to the others 'Frank is on his way.' Emily, her daughter Joan and daughter-in-law Pat (she married Geoff's brother Don), worked in the Frenchay Road establishment, named the Bungalow Tea Rooms. It was located on the riverside near the bridge that crosses the River Frome linking Frenchay Road with Pearces Hill and Frenchay Hill. The family lived in the bungalow next to the tea room, and it was at this rural location that Emily kept geese, chickens and pigs, with guard dogs to look after the property.

Disappointingly for Geoff the village school did not have an organised football team and he had to content himself with Friday afternoon football games when two teams were picked, coats put down for goalposts and matches maybe lasting several hours were enjoyed by the football-crazy lads. Attending Mangotsfield School (located in North View, Downend) from the age of 11 his football ability began to show as he was selected to play in the school's under-13s team in his first year at senior school – a fine achievement for such a young player and an indication of his burgeoning talent. Like most boys of his age at that time, Geoff left school at 14 and joined the world of employment, working as a driver's mate for a lemonade delivery firm, Keystones, in Fishponds. On his days off from delivering 'pop' bottles, football continued to play a significant part in his formative years.

One of his friends persuaded Geoff to play for a football team organised by Torchbearers, a Staple Hill club run by the Salvation Army Youth Club. Geoff's prowess at centre

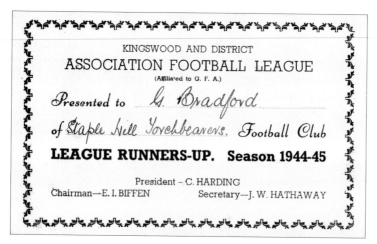

Certificate awarded to Geoff and members of the Torchbearers team for finishing as league runners-up in the 1944/45 season.

The Torchbearers Youth Football team were Kingswood & District Youth Challenge Cup Winners in 1943/44. Geoff Bradford, aged 17, is seated third from right.

Geoff, pictured right, and army pals, during his spell of National Service. He served with the Gloucestershire Regiment at Catterick, Colchester, Repton and Belfast.

forward was shown by him scoring the only goal of the final which helped the club win the Kingswood & District Youth Association Challenge Cup in 1944. The cup-winning celebration involved Geoff and his team-mates marching from Kingswood to Staple Hill proudly displaying the cup. Torchbearers enjoyed two successful seasons towards the end of the Second World War, winning the Challenge Cup and finishing as league runners-up in 1943/44 and were runners-up in both competitions the following season.

Geoff was a key member of that successful team in both of those seasons, riding his motorbike to the club for practice and matches. Some ten years later when nearing the pinnacle of his fame as a nationally known professional footballer, Geoff still found time to meet up with thirteen of his former Torchbearers team-mates at a reunion held in May 1953.

During the Second World War Geoff helped men to remove the railings that surrounded Frenchay church, ostensibly to be melted down in a morale-boosting drive to help the war effort. In 1945 between VE Day (8 May 1945) and VJ Day (15 August 1945) Geoff, then aged 18 years, was called up for National Service. The summons came a few weeks after the medical, delivered by the postman in a plain brown envelope, with the instruction that the prospective recruit had to report to barracks for the start of ten weeks of basic training. Geoff joined the Gloucestershire Regiment with whom he was initially stationed at Catterick in Yorkshire. Bradford, the young soldier, was later posted to Colchester, by which time he had been promoted to the rank of corporal in charge of corps training. Not particularly happy during his time spent in Essex, in an effort to temporarily get away Geoff volunteered with six others to undertake additional training on a small arms course in Warminster.

On returning to his unit Geoff was even more displeased when he discovered that his whole battalion had been flown out to the West Indies for a tour of duty. A six-month posting to Retford followed before moving to Belfast, this time as an NCO in charge of the demobilisation of young conscripted servicemen, who were leaving the armed forces. While in Ireland, football opportunities arose playing for his battalion team all over the country. During his time there he was invited for training by the Irish League Club, Bangor Town, after they spotted him playing in an army match, but they did not follow up their initial interest. His commanding officer, who had served in the Indian Army, was a keen hockey player and actively encouraged his charges to play the game. Geoff was selected for the battalion hockey team, once it was formed, with matches played on the barrack square after duties were completed. This was followed by evening football matches which really suited Geoff as a sports-loving teenager. Playing on the left wing Geoff excelled at hockey and was selected to represent Gloucestershire against Cheshire in the Army Hockey Cup final at Chester, where his team was beaten by a penalty. However, it was playing hockey that almost ended Geoff's football career before it had even started.

In one match he received a serious blow from an opponent's stick to the bridge of his nose and the corner of his right eye, which almost resulted in him losing the sight in that eye. Following this near miss he informed his CO that he did not want to risk another possible injury and decided not to play hockey again. While in the army Geoff

Geoff enjoyed army football and impressed in Ireland enough for Bangor Town to express an interest in him. He is second from right in the back row.

also participated in a number of athletics disciplines, winning a medal for the second place he achieved in a battalion long jump event in 1947. Geoff certainly enjoyed the army life which for him lasted for over 14 months, so much so that he seriously considered joining as a regular soldier and forging an army career. However, his battalion was spilt up and when his time came to be demobbed, he decided to return to Bristol and civvy street instead.

Geoff met Betty Flay, the young lady who was to become his wife, when he attended a local dance with some of his team-mates from Soundwell Football Club at Frenchay Village Hall one Saturday evening in 1949, a few weeks after his return from a trial with Blackpool Football Club. Betty, the daughter of Archibald and Ethel (née Roberts), at the time was living in Air Balloon Road, St George, and walked to the dance, a distance of nearly 4 miles, at some points having to walk across open fields to get to the venue. The couple were married on 19 February 1951 and had three children, all daughters; Lesley born in 1953, Lynn four years later in 1957 and Nichola, born in 1958. Like most Rovers professionals who were married, the Bradfords lived in a rented house owned by the football club close to the Eastville ground. The club also owned properties in the Brislington area of Bristol. Geoff and his young family lived at 57 Dormer Road, just off Muller Road in Eastville, a few hundred yards from Eastville Stadium, with team-mates Ray Mabbutt, Joe Davis and their families among other Rovers players who lived in 'club houses' in Dormer Road. Rovers directors, as did the manager, actively encouraged players to get married believing that a settled family life would improve their playing performance.

2

A CAREER IN PROFESSIONAL FOOTBALL

Following demobilisation from the army at the age of 20, and a return to his Frenchay home, Geoff joined his elder brother Don, a goalkeeper, at Soundwell Football Club, for whom he played at half-back as well as in the forward line. Soundwell, founded in 1936, who played home matches at the Star Ground, named after the nearby Star Inn public house located on the corner of Church Road and Soundwell Road, joined the Western League at the beginning of the 1945/46 season, but did not make an auspicious start finishing 13th out of 14 teams and conceding 132 goals in the process. The following season the club finished as Division Two runners-up, losing on just four occasions and scoring 111 goals, and entered the FA Cup for the first time. 1947/48 and 1948/49 saw Soundwell finish in 15th and 12th place respectively out of 18 teams conceding over 100 goals in both campaigns, but in 1948/49 the club had a good run in the FA Cup with a 9–3 win against Stonehouse followed by a 4–3 win at home to St Austell. In fact, the preliminary round victory by the odd goal in seven over the Cornish side on Saturday 18 September 1948 is the first printed reference so far discovered that reports Geoff Bradford's scoring prowess. The *Western Morning News* in its Monday report of the FA Cup tie had this to say, 'BRADFORD put Soundwell ahead after 17 minutes, but within three minutes Keast levelled the scores and then quickly gave the Cornish side the lead.' Glastonbury ended the Soundwell Wembley dream for another year, narrowly defeating the club 4–3 in the first qualifying round in October 1948. Don Bradford had already left Soundwell FC for Western League rivals Glastonbury, who in the immediate post-war period had a very successful side, finishing as runners-up in the Western League Division One in season 1947/48 and as champions the following season. The golden years for Glastonbury FC were a period of five seasons from 1947/48 to 1951/52 when the club won the Western League twice, were runners-up twice and third once. They also won the Somerset League twice and the Somerset Professional Cup. A particularly fine performance by Don came against Rovers' Colts in a Western League match at Eastville in December 1947, when despite conceding five goals the 1,500 spectators 'applauded Bradford for some magnificent saves'. The Rovers forwards were well on target in a side considerably strengthened by the inclusion of Petherbridge, Bush, Winters, Whitfield, Lockier and Liley who had all assisted in the Rovers Combination XI that season. On one occasion when Soundwell played Glastonbury, Geoff was called up to take a penalty against his brother, who promptly saved the spot-kick. However, the referee made the younger Bradford brother retake the penalty which Don duly saved again, but for a second time the referee spotted an infringement and ordered a third attempt. This time Geoff blasted the ball over the crossbar.

As well as a run in the early stages of the FA Cup in 1948/49, Soundwell also progressed in the FA Amateur Cup, beating Weston St John, Bristol St George, Hanham Athletic 4–2 in the second qualifying round, before going out of the competition in the next round, on 6 November, in a 3–1 home defeat to Clevedon. In the 3–2 qualifying round victory over Weston St John on Saturday 9 October 1948 the *Bristol Evening World* in its description of the first half of the game had this to report, 'Venning scored for St John when he sent the ball in from a corner. Within a short time BRADFORD put Soundwell on level terms. Soundwell pressed hard, but missed several opportunities at close range. Half-time: Weston St John 1 Soundwell 1.' A week later on 16 October, 'Soundwell played Bristol St George in the FA Amateur Cup, and triumphed by 3 goals to 2 on a rain-soaked pitch at Bell Hill. The home side were awarded a free kick when Bradford ran into Saints goalkeeper Jack Bright, but Soundwell took the lead after 12 minutes, when Bradford beat Bright from 20 yards.'

Geoff's performances for Soundwell in the Western League and cup competitions soon brought representative honours to the burgeoning star, when he was selected to play at inside right for the Gloucestershire Amateur Football Association against Birmingham & District County FA at Moor Green, Birmingham. The match, on Saturday 30 October, resulted in a 2–1 victory for the Gloucestershire side with Moserop and Greatbanks scoring for the visitors. On 4 December 1948 the Gloucestershire FA held a county trial game at Stonehouse to select their team to play against Berks and Bucks the following Saturday at Chesham. Geoff played for the Probables against the Possibles and is reported as having 'tried hard with an individual effort' in a 0–0 draw. Selected to represent the county in their Southern Counties Amateur Championship match on Saturday 11 December, Bradford's Gloucestershire team were defeated 3–0.

Geoff's scoring feats for Soundwell soon caught the attention of First Division Blackpool's West Country scout, and he was invited to Lancashire for a trial over the weekend of 18/19 December 1948. A well-established First Division club, Blackpool had many famous and talented footballers and Bradford was understandably very excited about this first opportunity to fulfil his ambition to become a professional footballer. Impressing in his trial, Geoff was signed as an amateur player by the Seasiders, but despite scoring 16 goals from inside forward in the Blackpool third team during a six-week trial period, he was not offered a professional contract. In practice games Geoff sometimes featured in the same forward line as Blackpool's international forward stars Stan Matthews and Stan Mortensen who were convinced that Geoff would be offered a contract. 'They both told me that I was bound to be retained,' he recalled, but unfortunately for Bradford it was not a view shared by Blackpool's manager, former England forward Joe Smith who had made 492 appearances for Bolton and captained the FA Cup-winning side of 1923, at the first Wembley FA Cup final. For a player who had scored 254 league goals for Bolton, Smith might have been expected to recognise the promise of the raw goalscoring talent from Bristol. However, it appears that he did not even take the trouble to have a look at the promising player in action. After greeting Bradford when he arrived at the Bloomfield Road ground, the next time he saw him was six weeks later when his only words to the crestfallen Bradford was to say, 'Cheerio lad, Keep in touch.' It had a profound effect on the aspiring professional footballer, 'I was a failure when I first tried to get into league football,' he recalled years later, 'Blackpool had me on trial and I played in about seven matches and scored 15 or 16 goals.'

Before leaving Blackpool Geoff was invited for another trial, this time with Blackburn Rovers, recently relegated from the First Division, but disheartened by his experience at Blackpool he initially refused the offer, saying that he wanted to go back to Bristol to think about it. His return to local football was deemed to be a newsworthy event as the *Bristol Evening World* in its report of the Soundwell v Trowbridge Town match played on 26 February 1949 had this to say, 'The appearance of Geoff Bradford, who has been in company with Matthews and Mortensen at Blackpool added thrust to the Soundwell attack,' but not enough as Soundwell were beaten 4–1. The paper also reported that Cliff Bryant, official scout for West Bromwich Albion was present watching a Soundwell player. After the end of the Second World War the standard of many top amateur clubs

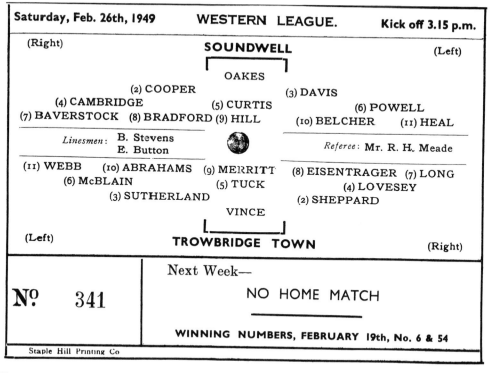

Team line-ups in the programme for the Western League match between Soundwell and Trowbridge Town at the Star Ground on 26 February 1949. Playing inside right it was Bradford's first game after returning from a six week trial at Blackpool.

was similar to the professional clubs. Numerous players preferred to work at a job rather than become a professional footballer as the maximum wage for players at the time was £8 per week. Spectators paid to watch Soundwell's home matches, entering the ground through one of four entrances, where they received a cloakroom ticket from one of the club members stationed with a card-table to take the fans' money. In a period when the sound of rattles and bells were prominent at football matches, an official programme, produced by Soundwell FC Supporters' Club, cost 2d each in 1948. Transport to away fixtures was provided by local coach firm the Princess Mary Motor Coaches of Soundwell Road, known locally as 'Wiltshire's', after the proprietor S.G. Wiltshire. A limited number of supporters were also able travel in the team coach, and the trip to Trowbridge in March 1948 was advertised at a fare of 6s. Soundwell also ran a second side known as Soundwell Athletic, named thus to circumvent the Bristol & District's League rule that club's reserves weren't permitted to compete in the league. Soundwell brought off several fine performances in the 1948/49 season, and proof of their work can be gauged from their Western League record. They averaged a point per match, which for an all-amateur side competing against largely professional opposition was not bad going.

Having played a couple more games for Soundwell on his return home from Blackpool, Geoff then decided to accept Blackburn's offer of a trial after all, the opportunity and his desire to become a professional footballer helping to diminish the memory of how let down he had felt at his treatment on his previous visit north. However, despite scoring more than a dozen goals for Blackburn's Colts side, Geoff once again faced rejection and was not taken on by the Ewood Park management. An interesting insight into the restrictions placed on footballers during the period is provided by one of one rules listed in the 'Player's Ticket' issued to the young Bradford during his short stay at Ewood Park. 'Players must not attend Dance Halls after Monday evening, except with special permission of the Trainer.'

Turning out once more for Soundwell in Division One of the Western League (who finished in 12th position out of 18 teams in 1948/49), playing against among others, Colts sides from both Bristol clubs – his continued good form brought Geoff a third trial offer, this time from Bristol City, who wanted him to play centre-half

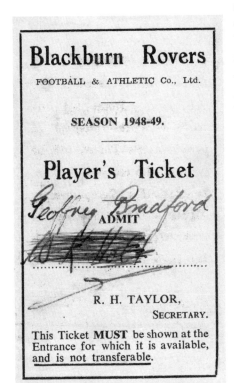

Geoff had unsuccessful trials at both Blackpool and Blackburn Rovers during 1948/49. A page from his player's ticket while at Ewood Park is pictured.

in their reserve side. Although still feeling disillusioned about Football League clubs in general and his treatment in particular, he declined the Ashton Gate club's invitation primarily because he did not want to miss any games in the Gloucestershire FA Senior Amateur competition in which Soundwell were doing well and who had an important cup tie that same afternoon. The club had reached the final of the prestigious local cup competition at the end of season 1947/48 only to be defeated 3–1 by Hambrook at Eastville Stadium on 1 May in front of a crowd of 5,795. Soundwell had progressed to the 1948 Senior Amateur Cup final by beating the likes of RAF Filton (7–6), Patchway Sports (5–0), Westbury Old Boys (7–2) after a replay, Beaufort United (4–2 following a 2–2 draw), and Bristol St George (3–2) on 6 March at Bell Hill in the semi-final after being 2–1 down at half time. The attendance at the match was 2,305 with gate receipts of £52 14s. Geoff was hoping that he could help them go one better and take the trophy in 1949. Soon after his rejection of City's trial offer he gave the same response to Bristol Rovers' chief scout, Wally Jennings, who wanted him to play for the reserves in a Football Combination game against Aldershot in April.

Then, however, a combination of circumstances led to Bradford eventually becoming a Pirate rather than a Robin. Winning against Marshfield Sports (2–1), St Pancras (4–1 after a 2–2 home draw), Bristol Trams (3–0), and Horfield Old Boys (5–1) in early rounds, and beating Mount Hill Enterprise 5–2 in the semi-final at Douglas' Ground in March – a game in which Bradford didn't score – Soundwell duly reached the final of the GFA Senior Amateur Cup (South) in May at Eastville Stadium in front of 8,631 spectators – a new record for Bristol amateur soccer. Soundwell won the cup for the first time in their history with the 5–0 defeat of Hanham Athletic of the Bristol & District League, who were thoroughly outclassed by a team which produced one of the best displays given by a Bristol amateur side for many a long year. Both individually and collectively, Soundwell were streets ahead and gave Hanham a lesson in tactics and ball control, particularly the latter which was of high standard on hard ground. Soundwell, whose Western League experience undoubtedly stood them in good stead, had a big pull at half-back, where Bradford, Curtis and Powell held complete control in midfield, and Soundwell's forwards received tremendous support from the halves, a trio of constructive half-backs, who blotted out the Hanham forwards. 'Bradford, a good two-footed player, always used the ball well and along with Powell provided their forwards with a wealth of openings.' And it was Geoff who put Soundwell ahead after three minutes, striking with a long shot against the inside of the upright, the ball then going over the line, following an indirect free kick awarded to Soundwell. Hill 2 (1 penalty), Williams and Harry Belcher were Soundwell's other scorers. Bob Lethaby, chairman of the GFA, presented the cup and medals to the winners, and a great celebration followed after the match at the Star Inn. Watched by the Rovers manager Brough Fletcher and Wally Jennings, Rovers' chief scout, the pair approached Bradford again after the match, this time with the offer of a contract and Geoff duly accepted the terms offered by Fletcher. Geoff had received a letter from local rivals Bristol City offering him a trial at Ashton Gate leading up to the final but advised City he wanted to get that game over before coming for the trial. He recalled in 1990 that he never received any further contact from the Ashton Gate club, but had kept their letter all those years. One can only now reflect on what a strike force might have been formed had John Atyeo and Geoff Bradford played in the same team.

So in June 1949, a month before his 22nd birthday, Geoff Bradford joined Bristol Rovers as a full-time professional earning £7 a week if selected for the first team, £5 in the reserves. The young Bradford had yet to even see a league game, never mind play in one! The official announcement of the club's new signings for the next season was made by Rovers' vice-chairman Mr John Hare at the annual gathering of the Supporters' Club at the All Hallows Hall, Easton, on 30 June. Geoff was described to the excited fans who attended the meeting thus, 'Geoff Bradford, centre-half, age 21 height 6ft, weight 12st 7lb has been signed as a full-time professional. He is [a] local who created a most favourable impression when playing right-half for Soundwell in the Senior Amateur Cup Final.' Another summer signing was Soundwell team-mate Tony Curtis, making, with Bryan Bush and Len Hodges, a total of four former Soundwell players at Eastville. In all, Rovers had 100 players on their books, 36 of whom were full-time professionals, with 28 of them Bristol-born. 'No other club can approach this percentage,' stated Rovers secretary John Gummow, 'and of the 36 it is an incredible fact that 29 had only one league club – Bristol Rovers.' Manager Brough Fletcher, the former Barnsley forward, who had played for, coached, and managed the Yorkshire club, had arrived at Eastville in January 1938, but was now in what were to be his last months with Rovers. The team reported back for training on Monday 25 July and under the watchful eye of Bert Tann, their coach, the players spent part of the morning doing some mild limb-loosening in the sunshine. 'They would see the ball on Thursday,' he informed. And so began the professional football career of Geoffrey Bradford. Trial matches commenced at Eastville on 6 August for sixty-one players – mostly amateurs, but including some of the new professionals – with the senior trial starting at 3.00 p.m. with Bradford at right-half in the Whites team alongside three former Soundwell players. By the time of the final trials a week later, which 5,500 spectators paid to watch, Bradford led the attack for the Whites in the second half of the senior trial, and soon helped to increase the 2–1 lead, when from his header goalwards Ray Warren deflected the ball into his own net. Bradford might have got another a

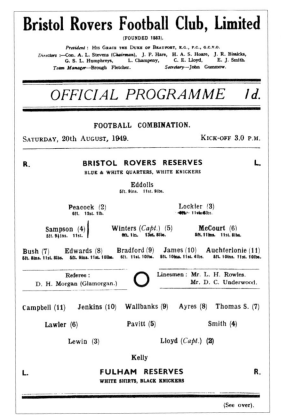

Programme dated 20 August 1949, for Bradford's debut for Rovers reserves against Fulham reserves which drew a crowd of 4,846 to Eastville. The game resulted in a 1–0 win for Rovers, the goal scored by Peter Sampson.

minute later had he been a fraction quicker in shooting, but he was always dangerous in the centre and received plenty of service from Ralph Jones and Alex Auchterlonie. The *Bristol Evening World* remarked, 'This is indeed an interesting experiment,' as although regarded as a half-back, 'he justified his inclusion, well built with a good shot.' Bradford was beginning to make his mark.

Indeed, Rovers employed him in the reserves as centre forward when he made his debut for them on Saturday 20 August against Fulham at Eastville in the opening Football Combination match of the season in front of 4,846 spectators. They generated gate receipts of £220 5s and a further £7 12s 7d was realised through the sale of 1,927 single-sheet programmes each costing 1d. A total of 585 season ticket-holders were included in the final attendance figure, while the remaining 4,261 spectators either paid 1s for entry to the ground, 1s 6d to watch from the enclosure or 2s to sit in the stand, while a total of 781 juvenile supporters paid their 6d to get in. Bradford, one of two newcomers in the side, headed into the hands of Hugh Kelly in the first minute, and at the next home attack he was warmly cheered for a quick shot which the goalkeeper cleared. In an eventful debut Bradford worried Kelly and was brought down by the Fulham goalkeeper. A penalty was awarded, which Bradford shot straight at Kelly, then in a further mêlée minutes later both players were knocked flat, and Kelly went off with an injured shoulder. The visitors, handicapped by the loss of their goalkeeper, were beaten by the only goal of the game, scored by Peter Sampson. The *Western Daily Press* had this to say about the new, well-built Rovers centre, 'Experience will improve Bradford. At present he does not use his height to advantage in the air.'

Playing in his preferred position in only his second reserve team match four days later, against Reading reserves in the Football Combination, Geoff scored his first ever hat-trick for the club in the 3–2 away win at Elm Park. The win

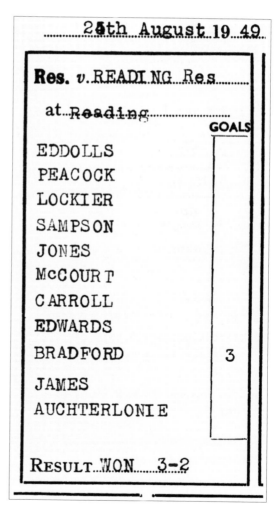

......24th August 19 49...

Res. *v.* READING Res...........

at..Reading....................

	GOALS
EDDOLLS	
PEACOCK	
LOCKIER	
SAMPSON	
JONES	
McCOURT	
CARROLL	
EDWARDS	
BRADFORD	3
JAMES	
AUCHTERLONIE	

RESULT..WON......3–2

Rovers team from the official match report against Reading reserves on 24 August 1949, recording Bradford's first goals for the Pirates – a hat-trick.

CRYSTAL PALACE

Claret and Blue Shirts, White Shorts

Graham

2 George   3 Dawes

4 Lewis   5 Watson   6 Chilvers

7 Clelland   8 Kurz   9 Rooke   10 Gaillard   11 Hanlon

Any changes in the teams will be announced on the loud speaker

Referee:
G. L. ILIFFE
(LEICS)

Linesmen:
B. M. Field
H. Redstall

Kick-off 3.15 p.m.

Watling 11   Bradford 10   Lambden 9   Hodges 8   Bush 7

McCourt 6   Warren 5   Pitt 4

Fox 3   Bamford 2

Weare

BRISTOL ROVERS

Shirts: Royal Blue & White Quarters, Shorts: White

8

The team line-ups from the Crystal Palace programme dated 24 September 1949 for Bradford's league debut.

was a personal triumph for Bradford who netted all the Rovers goals, two before and one after the interval. Two further reserve games without scoring were followed by a hat-trick for Rovers' Western League side against Bath City reserves at Bristol St George's ground and Rovers' only goal in a 4–1 defeat at Street. Recalled to the reserves at inside right for matches against Cardiff and Leyton Orient on 12 and 17 September respectively, progress was rapid and once Rovers manager Fletcher saw his potential, it was not long before he was selected for his first team debut. 'Bradford has deserved his quick promotion. Originally a wing-half he has made a success of playing at inside forward. He is tall and strong, and is quite a good player. He may lack experience, but when I saw him a week or two ago he showed appreciation of the cross-field pass in keeping both wingers well supplied. He has already figured among the goals on several occasions this season,' wrote a *Bristol Evening World* reporter.

His senior debut came on Saturday 24 September 1949 at Crystal Palace, where Rovers suffered a 1–0 defeat, Bradford supporting Vic Lambden at centre forward with Josser Watling outside him on the left wing and two former Soundwell players – Bush and Hodges – on the right of the front line. It was a quiet debut for the new Pirate although Bradford did have one chance when Vic Lambden raced out to the wing and centred. It was only a split-second chance, but he put it over the bar. The Bristol press reported that they could see potential in the converted half-back, 'Bradford had a good first appearance in the Rovers team. He shot at goal at every available opportunity. And he has the look of a potential match-winner,' wrote the *Bristol Evening World*, while the *Bristol Evening Post* felt that, 'He may have to learn the hard way. He had the chances that a more experienced man might have capitalised. He deserves another chance.'

Geoff had replaced Tony James at inside left in the struggling Rovers team which lay in bottom position of Division Three (South) but kept his place to enable him to make his home debut at Eastville the following Saturday, when Watford left with a 2–0 victory. Not the best of starts for the young Bradford and in the circumstances it was hardly surprising that he failed to make an immediate impact. He was then rested as James was recalled to the first team. Bradford was finding it difficult to score in the Rovers reserve team, although he did manage two goals in a 12–0 victory over the University of Bristol in a friendly played at the university's sports ground at Coombe Dingle on 27 October. Two more

One of the earliest photos of Bradford training with Rovers at Eastville in 1949.

goals in the Western League, against Poole Town and Clandown in November were followed by a single strike in the 5–4 Combination win at Luton. However, a run in the reserve side at the start of 1950 resulted in a Bradford goalscoring run which commenced on 7 January, a few days after the sacking of Rovers' manager Brough Fletcher. It began with two goals in a 6–0 win over Cardiff at Eastville, followed by single strikes against Plymouth Argyle twice and Bournemouth at Dean Court at the beginning of February. The departure of manager Fletcher in January with Rovers in seventeenth place (having gained only 19 points from 23 games) and the appointment of coach Bert Tann as his replacement was fortunate for Bradford as he was given a run in the first team by the new manager. In his fifth league appearance of the season, on 4 March 1950, Geoff scored his first ever senior goal for Rovers at Walsall in a 3–1 defeat. His equalising goal within a few minutes of Walsall's opener, a brilliant effort taken with the cool precision of a much more experienced player, was the best goal of the match. Confronted by two defenders on the edge of the penalty area, he calmly took stock of the situation and lobbed the ball out of the goalkeeper's reach into the corner of the net. More than once during the match he beat three opponents in a dazzling dribble that took him nearly half the length of the field.

On this form, the Bristol press considered that Bradford was here to stay. 'Geoff Bradford took the eye with considerable force when he played against Watford in place of injured Tony James a week ago, and he played even better on Saturday. With Geoff the craftsman is already there. He only lacks experience, and he is catching up with that deficiency very rapidly. He is tall and strong, and I like the rapidity with which he switches position and the speed and force with which he shoots. In fact if Saturday's form is to be a regular thing, I will go so far as to say that the Rovers have no inside forward problem – always provided, of course, that the development of this young player progresses at its present rate,' wrote an *Evening Post* reporter. Geoff retained his place for the final thirteen matches

1st XI v.	Walsall	GOALS
at	Walsall	
Goal ...	Liley	
R.B. ...	Bamford	
L.B. ...	Fox	
R.H. ...	Pitt	
C.H. ...	Warren	
L.H. ...	McCourt	
O.R. ...	Petherbridge	
I.R. ...	Bradford	1
C.F. ...	Lambden	
I.L. ...	Roost	
O.L. ...	Bush	
RESULT	Lost 1 - 3	

Part of Rovers' official match report for games played on 4 March 1950 records Bradford's first senior goal for the club. The first of 242 league goals scored in his career.

Five-year-old mascot Tony Spiller leads Rovers out at Eastville on 11 March 1950 before the game against Millwall, accompanied by captain Ray Warren. Geoff Fox, Bryan Bush, Frank McCourt, Geoff Bradford and Vic Lambden follow their skipper.

A cartoon drawn by Pak for that Millwall match at Eastville which Rovers won 3–1.

Bradford waits to see if the opposition goalkeeper fails to collect the ball watched by team-mate George Petherbridge far right, during a game at Eastville.

of that season, adding two more goals, netting the solitary winning goal against Exeter City on 10 April and contributed another in the emphatic 5–1 win over Norwich City two weeks later, both at Eastville.

After a poor start to the season with just two wins in their first ten league games Rovers improved and eleven wins in the first nineteen league games under Bert Tann enabled Rovers to finish in ninth place with 43 points, a respectable end to the 1949/50 league season. Leading scorer was Bill Roost with 13 goals, 7 ahead of Vic Lambden. Bradford, one of six debutants during that season, scored 3 goals in 18 league appearances. There might have been another goal if goalkeeper Jack Ansell had not just managed to punch the ball away as Bradford was about to head it in during a scoreless Eastville draw with Northampton. On 13 May Geoff experienced his first ever local derby against Bristol City when Rovers were defeated 2–0 at Ashton Gate in the annual Gloucestershire FA Senior Cup final. It was the first of 29 league and cup encounters with arch-rivals City that Bradford played in during his long career. To compliment his three league goals in his first season as a professional, Bradford added nine Football Combination goals, and six against Western League opposition.

One of the major turning points in the history of Bristol Rovers was the appointment of Bertram James Tann as manager early in January 1950. The new manager had arrived, as a coach at Eastville, on the personal recommendation of Sir Stanley Rous, then Secretary of the Football Association, and also of Cliff Lloyd, later the Secretary of the Professional

Manager Bert Tann discusses team tactics with, from left to right: Geoff Bradford, Josser Watling, Peter Sampson, Bryan Bush, Harry Bamford, Jackie Pitt, Bert Tann, Ray Warren.

Footballers' Association and once a Rovers reserve player. Tann, a charismatic 45-year-old Londoner who had played professional football with Charlton Athletic, breathed new life into Brough Fletcher's side. He forged close working links with the local community through schools and organisations and established pre-season training camps at Uphill, Weston-super-Mare, where Rovers teams fostered close relationships and these were to be significant gatherings in boosting morale. Tann's eighteen years as manager were to see Rovers reach two FA Cup quarter-finals as well as the distant dreamland of Division Two.

Although the decision to sack Fletcher had been a unanimous one, it provoked a rift between directors, which was to plague Rovers for a number of months. Tann's task, as his replacement, was to convert a team of local players and free-transfer signings into a side capable of holding its own in Division Three (South) and subsequently in Division Two. Tann certainly inherited very settled defensive and half-back lines, where Harry Bamford and Geoff Fox continued to be models of reliability at full-back, with Fox and centre-half Ray Warren ever-presents and right-half Jackie Pitt missing only two games during 1949/50. However, no forward appeared in more games than Roost, whose 28 appearances in 42 league matches made him stand out in attack. During the summer of 1950, the board had waived its 'No Buy, No Sell' policy to allow two transfers to take place. Goalkeeper Bert Hoyle was signed from Exeter City for £350, while Frank McCourt was sold for £2,000 to Manchester City, where he won six Northern Ireland caps. Len Hodges moved on a free transfer to Swansea Town, while veteran wing-half Wally McArthur retired to become assistant trainer.

3

CUP GLORY AND A CHAMPIONSHIP MEDAL

For the 1950/51 season, while Rovers' financial affairs continued to come under scrutiny from the Football Association and the Board of Trade, the side's performances on the field under manager Bert Tann still impressed. Sixth place in Division Three (South) was a fine end-of-season position and a first-ever FA Cup quarter-final, through a cup run which earned the club £5,754, was a major achievement.

In his second season Bradford played regularly, forming an effective goalscoring partnership with Vic Lambden, an ever-present who top scored with 20 goals in his 46 league matches. Bradford managed 15 goals in 37 appearances and was second highest scorer with Bill Roost netting 7 times. In fact, Bradford appeared in 49 of the 60 senior games including all 11 FA Cup ties. That season is, of course, primarily remembered for the scintillating FA Cup run which took the club further in the competition than ever before. Geoff, when interviewed at the time, recalled that the 'muddy pitch at Eastville was our big ally. I remember once we were standing in the tunnel as the ref inspected the pitch and someone said if he doesn't sink down to his knees the game is on. Part of our training used to be dragging a sheet of galvanised tin, weighed down by a couple of players standing on it, over the mud to flatten it. Things like that helped to a build up a great team spirit.'

The Rovers Supporters' Club was rapidly expanding and with fans wanting more social events, regular dances were arranged at the Berkeley Café in Clifton which were well attended by the Rovers players and staff. Fundraising for the club was significant by those fans, who contributed to the substantial expenditure required to provide facilities at Eastville Stadium for themselves and the players. As the team became successful, the supporters' club arranged for thousands of fans to travel by train and coaches to away matches. In what was a rarity in professional football at the time, manager Tann provided film coverage of the matches to show the players how to improve tactical awareness and player performance.

Rovers' cup exploits fired the imagination of the success-starved Bristol sporting public. That season the FA Cup ensured plenty of excitement for the players and supporters. The run was slow in starting, for Rovers required three games to dispose of non-league Llanelly in the first round. Rovers and Llanelly each played in eleven FA Cup matches in 1950/51, more than any other competing club. The Welsh side boasted Jock Stein, later an influential international manager with Scotland, at centre-half. Once Rovers had won the second replay 3–1 at Ninian Park, they still required three more games before disposing of

Bristol Rovers first team, 1950/51.
Back row, left to right: Jackie Pitt, Barry
Watkins, Harry Bamford, Bert Hoyle, Geoff
Fox, Peter Sampson, Bert Williams (trainer).
Front row: Bryan Bush, Geoff Bradford,
Vic Lambden, Ray Warren (captain), Jimmy
Morgan, Josser Watling.

Geoff looks to start another Rovers attack
during a match in the early 1950s.

Gillingham 2–1. Bradford recalled in an interview given in 1986 that, on scoring the vital second goal against Llanelly he had help following some gamesmanship from team-mate Bill Roost. This was something he repeated in one of the three more games while disposing of Gillingham 2–1 in appalling weather at White Hart Lane. Geoff recounted:

> Roost used to kick up a rumpus with the referee when we were awarded free kicks. Insisting the defensive wall was too close and shouting instructions to all and sundry. I would stand close to him but looking as if I was not taking much notice. Then Bill tapped a quick kick to me to whip the ball into the net while everything was still in a state of confusion as a result of Bill's antics. We felt we could not make such hard work of getting through the second round. But again we were held at Eastville in a 2–2 draw and were lucky not to lose the replay at Gillingham.

In the third match of the tie played at neutral Tottenham, Ray Warren converted a penalty 5 minutes from time to secure victory and progression to the next round. Only 10,000 spectators, Rovers' lowest home crowd of the season, saw the third round clash with Aldershot, but once Vic Lambden had given Rovers the lead after only 8 seconds, it was a comfortable 5–1 victory which included a Lambden hat-trick.

Over 26,000 saw Rovers win at Second Division Luton Town in the next round, George Petherbridge scoring the winning goal. Cup fever now gripped Bristol and a new ground record of 31,660, producing receipts of £2,600, gathered at Eastville for the visit of Hull City. The Second Division visitors fielded the veteran former England international Raich Carter and the future England manager Don Revie as their inside forwards. Two goals from Josser Watling ensured Rovers enjoyed a convincing 3–0 victory and a place in the quarter-finals of the FA Cup for the first time in the club's history. Watling's first

Bristol Rovers were featured on the front cover of *Sport* magazine in February 1951. Back row, left to right: Jackie Pitt, Harry Bamford, Bert Hoyle, Geoff Fox, Vic Lambden, Peter Sampson. Front row: George Petherbridge, Geoff Bradford, Ray Warren, Geoff Roost, Josser Watling.

followed a goalmouth scramble after 26 minutes and his second, 10 minutes after half time, crashed in off the crossbar. A quarter of an hour from time, victory was sealed when Roost set up Lambden for the third. On Monday 12 February 1951, the Rovers players went down to the *Bristol Evening Post* offices to watch the sixth round draw being recorded on a teleprinter machine, which brought great excitement when Rovers were paired with First Division giants Newcastle United. The unexpected but welcome progress in the FA Cup, however, put Geoff Bradford in a bit of a predicament because, not having expected the club to be involved in the latter stages of the competition, he had arranged to marry fiancée Betty Flay on the Monday before the date of the sixth round tie. Before the wedding arrangements had been finalised Geoff explained to her the snags of marrying a footballer in the season, but even he had not bargained on still being concerned with the FA Cup at such a late stage in the competition. However, manager Bert Tann gave him permission to go ahead with the wedding. The couple attempted to keep the event at Christ Church, Downend, on 19 February a private affair, but hundreds of Rovers supporters turned up outside the church to see the couple married, and all the team attended the ceremony before going off for special training at Southend-on-Sea.

The newly-wed Bradford joined them after being permitted to stay behind for a one-day honeymoon. The new Mrs Bradford then joined the other players' wives in linking up with the Rovers party on Friday, staying at Whitley Bay while in the north-east, prior to the team's sixth round tie at Newcastle.

On 24 February 1951 Rovers defended superbly for a goalless draw with Newcastle United in the FA Cup quarter-final at St James' Park.

A large crowd of well wishers gathered outside of Christ Church, Downend, for the marriage of Geoff to Betty Flay on 19 February 1951.

Geoff and Betty raise a toast on the occasion of their wedding in February 1951.

Bradford crosses the ball at St James' Park on 24 February 1951 during the goalless draw with Newcastle United in the FA Cup quarter-final. The match was watched by over 63,000 fans including 5,000 from Bristol.

The attendance, 62,787, which produced £7,561 in gate receipts, remains the largest ever at a football match involving Rovers. Around 5,000 Rovers supporters had travelled to this remarkable game, and thousands of fans greeted the players when they returned by train to Bristol – three hours late owing to a Western Region strike – with the team's battle hymn 'Goodnight Irene'.

Following the game, Bert Tann, who had turned down around £90,000 in offers for players since he started the team on their record-breaking way, had this to say, 'Please tell the clubs with money to burn that we are just not interested in their dazzling cheques. When we were just another Third Division club nobody seemed over-anxious to increase our bank balance. Let the big fellows find their own players and leave us alone.'

Some 100,000 fans queued at Eastville two days later for tickets for the Wednesday afternoon replay. A considerable number of policemen were involved in keeping about 50,000 people out of the Eastville car park as soon as it became evident how quickly the tickets sold out. As it was, a number of businesses shut and children missed school as supporters without tickets tuned in to the live wireless commentary of the match and 30,074 excited fans crammed into Eastville for the game itself. The Eastville Roar was heard for the first time 15 minutes in, amid scenes of incredulous delight, when Geoff Bradford scored a fine opportunist goal to give Rovers a surprise lead. Bradford superbly drove the ball home left-footed when it ran loose following a centre from Bryan Bush, creating pandemonium in the ground, as the scorer recalled, 'But our elation proved to be our downfall. We were so excited at being ahead, and suddenly we were 1–3 down. We penned Newcastle back, but couldn't get another goal.'

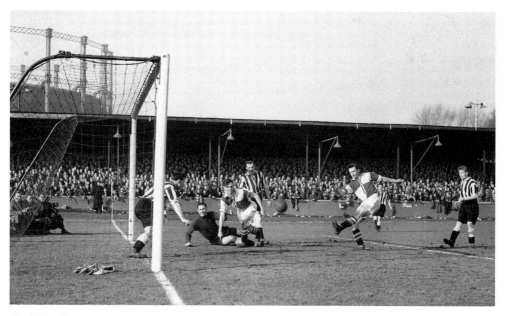

Geoff Bradford opens the scoring for Rovers against Newcastle United in the FA Cup sixth round replay at Eastville to the cheers of over 30,000 supporters.

By half time, goals from Ernie Taylor, whose shot deflected in off Geoff Fox, Charlie Crowe and the legendary Jackie Milburn, gave the Magpies victory, despite a spirited second-half Rovers revival. Newcastle United went on to win the cup with the same eleven players who had faced Rovers twice in four days by defeating Blackpool at Wembley. The preponderance of local talent in Rovers' team that afternoon was the underlying reason for their prosperity in those early years of the Tann regime. 'The strength of Rovers during the successful years of the 1950s was the marvellous team spirit at Eastville. We were proud to pull on a Rovers shirt and play for the club. That was what mattered most of all. We were doing something we dearly wanted to do, and we were getting paid for it too. Football was always a game to me first, a career second,' recalled Bradford years later.

Throughout the 1950/51 season, one key to Rovers' success was their ability to retain a consistent side. Apart from half a dozen players who appeared in no more than seven games each, Rovers relied on just twelve relatively regular players in the side. Goalkeeper Bert Hoyle, half-backs Ray Warren and Peter Sampson and top scorer Vic Lambden – the first post-war Rovers player to reach twenty league goals for the season – played in all 58 league, FA Cup and Gloucestershire Cup games. A settled defence was completed by full-backs Harry Bamford and Geoff Fox and right-half Jackie Pitt, who between them missed just nine league games all season. In the forward line, Geoff Bradford and Bill Roost ably supported Lambden, with Petherbridge, Watling and Bush competing for the remaining places.

Bill Roost, John McIlvenny, Geoff Bradford, Peter Hooper and Barrie Meyer help clear the Eastville terraces of winter snow.

In completing the season in sixth place, Rovers fell back on an excellent autumn run of nine wins and three draws. Following defeat at Norwich City in September, the side was unbeaten until going down 1–0 at Crystal Palace in January. Eastville was developing into a stronghold (between November 1949 and April 1953 only 5 home league games out of 81 were lost), where Rovers won 13 and drew 4 of their first 17 home league matches. Indeed, it was the penultimate league game before Rovers' proud unbeaten home record finally fell to runaway champions Nottingham Forest. There were five-figure crowds at every home match in 1950/51 at an average of 17,763, with the highest at a league game being the 31,518 that saw Lambden's double strike defeat Bristol City in December. As part of the Festival of Britain celebration, on 14 May Bradford featured at inside left in the match at Eastville against the Dutch side Racing Club Haarlem. The Festival of Britain in 1951 was a national exhibition of the cultural life of the British Isles, organised by the government to give Britons a feeling of recovery in the aftermath of war and to promote the British contribution to science, technology, industrial design, architecture and the arts. For the festival, many continental teams played against the best British teams, with 32 matches taking place over a 12-day period in May. Bradford's first taste of 'international' football ended in a 0–0 draw.

On the back of FA Cup success, Rovers built a side which would fulfil its potential in the spring of 1953. Manager Bert Tann had taken on successfully the task of maintaining Rovers' post-war promotion push with a consistent and efficient team that was riding high in Division Three (South) and had reached the FA Cup quarter-finals. The extent to which Rovers were relying on Lambden and Bradford for their goals was amply demonstrated by the fact that between them they totalled more than 60 in the 1951/52 season. Lambden led the way with 29 in the league and 4 in the FA Cup; Bradford scored 26 and 3 respectively. On the final day both were again on the mark in a home draw with Exeter City, Lambden's goal taking him to 100 for the club in league and cup, and Bradford's giving him an overall tally of 50. Undeniably, the fact that Rovers could boast two hugely prolific goalscorers was a key factor in the side's success. Lambden had proved his pedigree, but continued in fine style. His four goals against Colchester United made him the only player to have scored so many times twice in the league for Rovers. His club record 29 league goals in 1951/52 were followed by 24 more the following year when, as an ever-present, he helped Rovers towards great success.

Bradford, on the other hand, was just beginning to prove his worth as his 26 league goals included 10 in the final 8 games. Bradford did have his critics with some fans calling him lazy, but Bradford, known as 'Rip' (Van Winkle) to team-mates because of his knack for sleeping to conserve energy before a match, could justifiably refer them to his goal tally. Prior to the game at Brisbane Road on 6 February, Rovers and Leyton Orient observed a one-minute silence in memory of King George VI, who had died at Buckingham Palace the previous day. The match itself was very exciting with Bradford scoring twice for Rovers and Orient's half Jackie Deverall contributing an own goal as the sides shared six goals.

Autographed picture of Bradford that appeared in
Charles Buchan's Football Monthly *magazine.*

The 1952/53 season started well with eight league victories in the first twelve games followed by Rovers' remarkable run of twelve consecutive league victories. That magnificent record started on 18 October 1952 with a narrow 2–1 win over Leyton Orient at Eastville, followed by victories over Ipswich, Reading, Bournemouth, Southend, Brighton, Crystal Palace, Shrewsbury, QPR (twice), Walsall, and Gillingham. Just five goals were conceded in those twelve straight wins and 34 goals scored, with Bradford netting nine during that twelve-match run. On 24 January Millwall drew with Rovers at Eastville; The Lions in fact were the only club to take four points from Rovers during that memorable season as they finished as runners-up to the Pirates.

After defeat at Millwall on 13 September, Rovers embarked on a club record 27-match unbeaten run, after which the championship appeared won. Bradford scored a hat-trick in a 3–0 victory over Torquay United in September with three right-foot shots. Lambden, whose cross was so good that Bradford only had to sidefoot the ball past the diving Webber into the net, set up the first. And again it was Lambden who hooked the ball into the centre and again Bradford, after two Torquay defenders had swung at the ball and missed, was there to take advantage of the mistake. From a corner the ball was only partially cleared to Bradford, who made no mistake in completing his hat-trick. Despite playing in nine league matches during the month of September, Bradford found the time and energy to turn out for Rovers reserves on 22 September against Leicester City reserves, scoring a hat-trick in a 3–1 win. Bradford had cause for double celebration, professionally and in his family life during that momentous season. As he left the field on 31 January 1953 after scoring two goals against Aldershot, he was met by Bristol Rovers officials, who told him that his wife had just given birth to their first child, a daughter named Lesley Anne.

First Division Chelsea were among the top clubs reported to be after Bradford, and manager Bill Dodgin tried to sign him for Fulham, but in firmly turning down a bid by Liverpool in November 1952, Bert Tann made it clear, despite bids for Rovers players in the previous few months which had totalled well over £100,000, that 'we are determined more than ever that none of our lads shall leave. We want them all in our great effort to reach the Second Division.' Liverpool manager Don Welsh made the offer of between £22,000 and £25,000 for Bradford which had thrown the famous 'No Buy – No Sell' policy once again into the spotlight of national publicity. This bid would have constituted a record transfer fee for a Third Division player if it had been accepted – but Rovers stuck to their policy not to sell no matter how tempting the transfer fee offered. Bradford recalled another occasion,

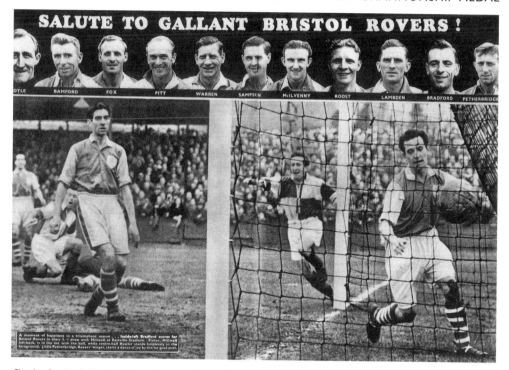

Charles Buchan's Football Monthly magazine salutes the Rovers team. The photograph shows Bradford's goal against Millwall at Eastville on 24 January 1953. Millwall challenged Rovers strongly for the Championship finishing the season as runners-up.

just before his first serious injury, when the Rovers players were out for a stroll on Plymouth Hoe before a game at Home Park. 'We spotted a scout from a First Division club known to be interested in Vic Lambden and me. He was signalling to the pair of us, trying to get us to separate from the others so that he could have a private word with Vic and me, but we stayed together with the group. I never thought of asking for a transfer. In those days of the maximum wage I was earning as much as I could in the Second Division and the increase for stepping up into the First was not all that much.' With the maximum wage in force for professional footballers, the top earner at Rovers was captain Ray Warren on £18 a week – a far cry from the salaries of modern football.

A fascinating insight for the Rovers fans who packed the terraces, into the regime behind the success on the field was provided in a *Bristol Evening World* article written in 1953 by Peter Barnes. Bert Tann, the Rovers manager who had groomed the players to stardom:

A footballer's life is an easy one, but not many people appreciate it is a seven days a week job. Every player is under the trainer's orders for 24 hours a day and seven days a week. We make that perfectly plain to every new player who joins us. So on Sunday mornings, before the cleaners have moved the litter of paper and orange peel from the terracing, the players are arriving back at the ground. Bert Williams, who has been trainer at Eastville for more than 30 years, likes them to call for another hot bath to ease their leg muscles. There's an oil massage for those with bruises and sprains, and electrical treatment for anybody with a more serious bruise. Monday is a day of relaxation for everyone, but the players turn up for hip baths in tepid water. Tuesdays they do their hard training of the week. They are kept going at top speed for up to 90 minutes. On Wednesdays it's free and easy exercises – heading tennis, punch-bag work, a game of golf at Filton, or a long walk in the country or at Weston-super-Mare. Mr Tann believes that variety in training keeps his players in the peak of condition. Thursday is another busy training day, and as on Tuesdays, they wind up with ball practice. Fridays you will find the Rovers strolling through Eastville Park, as their training for the week is over. But they are back at the Stadium by 11.00 a.m. for Tann to hold his weekly open court. Players can discuss any subject that they like, but Tann is unable to recall when there was last a grouse from anyone in the Rovers family circle. Tactics may be discussed and if the club's representative on the Players' Union has anything to report, this is the chance. Tann has no fads about diets for his players. He just likes them to have plenty of meat, and for that reason Rovers have their own canteen where the players have lunch six days a week. They even report there on match days, although instead of roast on Saturday, the menu is fish, cold mutton and toast. In the dressing-rooms you always find hot Horlicks or Bovril waiting for the players after training. On match days there is a box of glucose tablets on the table and weak tea to drink during the interval. Lemons and oranges fell from grace as the interval refreshment for players during the war when they were unobtainable. Soccer clubs haven't gone back to them. Mr Tann doesn't believe in giving a player alcoholic stimulants unless he has had a heavy knock on the head. 'Their bodies should be strong enough to stand blows, and cold water from the sponge should do the rest,' he adds. In the middle of every dressing-room you'll find a long, well-padded table where the trainer massages the injured limbs, 'which some of players avoid like the plague,' says Bert Williams, 'They regard it as a bad omen if they have to have treatment.' Every afternoon the players are free to do as they like, but nine of the Rovers players are married and odd jobs at home keep them busy. Mr Tann is glad he has so many married men, for he regards them as a steadying influence and good example to the younger players. Most of the players are cinema enthusiasts and it's not surprising. Three of the best-known cinemas in Bristol give each player two tickets a week.

By their deeds the eleven fit young men of Bristol Rovers were making their team a household name throughout the country with the claim to fame in those days when a footballer could cost a club anything up to £35,000, they cost under £1,000 in total – the cheapest team there was. Nine of them cost only a £10 signing-on fee and seven were Bristolians.

It seems implausible, but Rovers won just one of their final nine league matches, but still managed to hang on and win the Third Division (South) Championship. The sole victory, however, was the significant 3–1 victory at home to Newport County on 25 April, which secured promotion to Division Two. With impeccable timing, Bradford, having established a new club seasonal record at Somerton Park twelve days earlier, scored a majestic hat-trick to send the Pirates to the second tier of English football for the first time in their history. But it was not until half an hour before the kick-off that manager Bert Tann decided to play Bradford, delaying his decision until Rovers' inside left and top scorer with 31 goals, had been examined by the club's doctor. Although the ankle injury he received at Norwich on the Wednesday had improved, it was still a long way from having healed. But he wanted to play, and the club's doctor said playing would not aggravate the injury, although there might be pain. So onto the field ran Bradford with the team and within a minute he put the Rovers one up. From a second corner within moments of the start Roost's persistence gave him possession and Watling slammed the ball back for Bradford to score from an easy chance from close in.

A mighty roar rose from the 29,451 crowd to greet Bradford's 32nd goal of the season. Just 5 minutes from half time the Pitt/Bradford combination put Rovers ahead again, from a free kick taken 30 yards out; the wing-half placed his kick perfectly for Bradford to head over Harry Fearnley's head into the back of the net. Petherbridge's centre, in the 70th minute, was placed accurately and Bradford jumped high to head the ball into the corner of

The front page of the *Bristol Evening World*'s Saturday sports supplement *Pink 'Un*, dated 25 April 1953, proclaims 'They've Done It!' as Rovers achieve promotion.

the goal to complete his hat-trick. By then the Newport goalkeeper had left the field with a shoulder injury and replaced in the County goal by right-winger Cliff Birch. For the last 20 minutes Bradford was in throbbing pain and limping, but he had already done enough to make Rovers virtually sure of promotion. Although Northampton Town won their game that same afternoon and were only 2 points behind Rovers, they had only one game to play, and would need to win that 30–0 to stand a chance on goal average, even if Rovers lost their two remaining games.

Bradford had his ankle treated and bound just before kick-off and Bert Tann explained the decision he had had to make only a few minutes before the game started, 'It was a difficult one to make. On another occasion I might have played safe and put someone else in, but he wanted to play so badly and the game was important, I decided to take a chance. You know what happened – it made his performance a truly great one,' he said. Bradford's display was typical of Rovers' terrific fighting ability, grim determination and wonderful spirit. Everyone was in back-slapping mood afterwards as champagne corks popped, and goodwill telephone messages poured in. As he eased his left foot tenderly into his sock, Bradford said, 'I hope I'm OK by Wednesday. We play Aldershot and I don't want to miss it.' He did make the side for the goalless away draw at Aldershot but with promotion confirmed was rested for the final league game, a 1–0 defeat at Crystal Palace.

In an interesting finale to the history-making season a crowd of nearly 12,000 streamed into Badminton Park, the home of Rovers' president, the Duke of Beaufort, by road and rail to watch Rovers defeat First Division opponents Cardiff City 3–1 in a charity friendly match. Although there was a doubt about Bradford's injured heel, he was so keen to turn out that manger Bert Tann gave in to him. At probably what was one of the most unusual venues in his professional career, improvised stands were erected with carts and wagons placed end to end round the three sides of the enclosure, with the 'press box' the farm cart used by the queen on one of her recent visits to the Badminton Horse Trials. The match was filmed by Pathé News and highlights were included in their cinema news presentation. In what must be a unique half-time entertainment for a Rovers match, the crowd were treated to a parade of the Duke of Beaufort's hounds during the interval. Afterwards the players, their wives, and officials of both clubs were the guests of the Duke and Duchess of Beaufort at a buffet supper in one of the state rooms of Badminton House. Their graces personally attended to the needs of Geoff and Betty and the rest of their guests, the whole occasion was delightfully informal, besides being a unique event.

The Rovers Supporters' Club laid on a formal dinner for the promotion-winning side at the Berkeley Café, Queen's Road, Clifton, on Friday 15 May 1953. Rovers chairman Herbert Hampden Alpass received the Championship shield and thirteen medals at a Football League meeting held at the Café Royal in London on 13 June.

The players divided a £275 bonus between them for their achievement. All of the first team players were paid the maximum wage of £14 a week – just like the players of Arsenal, Newcastle United, and Manchester United. Only two players on Bristol Rovers' books had cost more than the regulation £10 signing-on fee – goalkeeper Bert Hoyle and right-winger John McIlvenny.

The Lord Mayor and the Lady Mayoress

request the pleasure of the company of

Mr. Bradford and Lady

at a Reception at the Mansion House,

on Tuesday the 12th of May, 1953,

to celebrate the Bristol Rovers winning the Championship

of the Football League, Third Division (South).

Kindly reply to
The Lord Mayor's Secretary,
The Council House, Bristol, 1.

7.30 till 9 p.m.
Informal Dress

Rovers' championship-winning squad and their wives were invited by the Lord Mayor of Bristol to a reception at the Mansion House on 12 May 1953.

The obverse of Geoff Bradford's 1953 Division Three (South) Championship medal.

Although he scored just twice, McIlvenny, like George Petherbridge on the left, was instrumental in creating many of Rovers' club record 92 league goals. In both cases all that was paid – £350 for Hoyle and £400 for McIlvenny – was the amount of the players' accrued share of benefit. A footballer was paid a benefit of up to £750 for every five years' service with any club. On transfer from one club to another he was entitled to draw that amount of benefit he had earned during his period of service with his original club.

Rovers' arrival in Division Two was announced with a hugely entertaining 4–4 draw with Fulham at Craven Cottage on the evening of Thursday 20 August 1953 in a rare midweek start to the league season. In predictable fashion, Geoff Bradford opened the scoring after 13 minutes when he ran the ball into the net from a Petherbridge centre following a fine run by Meyer and marked the occasion with a hat-trick, adding a second in the 57th minute after Petherbridge had a shot only partially cleared, and his third, the best goal of the game, with 15 minutes remaining when he steered Watling's cross into the net with a perfect header. Geoff Fox, 4 minutes after half time, scored only his second goal in over 200 appearances. The Rovers' start to their Second Division life was all the more encouraging because it was felt doubtful whether they would be called upon to meet stiffer opposition or a team that had better inside forwards than Bobby Robson, Bedford Jezzard and Johnny Haynes. Such was the interest in the game that the *Bristol Evening Post* reported that more than 300 telephone calls were put through to their offices on the night of the game by anxious soccer fans who wanted to know the result of Rovers' first-ever Second Division match. Many calls came from local clubs and public houses, and when callers were told that the Rovers had drawn 4–4 with Fulham there was cheering and wild speculation about their chances of winning

Rovers' complete playing squad and officials pose with the Third Division (South) Championship Shield after their first ever promotion in season 1952/53. Geoff Bradford is seated third from the right in the front row.

the Division Two championship. Some people said they had tried to ring the Fulham ground in London, but could not get through because the number was engaged. Many rang from villages and towns throughout North Somerset and South Gloucestershire, with supporters beginning to ring at half time (7.15) and were still ringing at 11.00 p.m. The star attraction, once again, was the phenomenal goalscorer Bradford, who followed up his club record 33 league goals in 1952/53 with 21 goals in only 18 league appearances in 1953/54. Further hat-tricks followed against Brentford, Notts County, Luton Town and Stoke City. By the end of October Bradford had no fewer than five senior hat-tricks to his name since the start of the season, four scored for the Rovers and notching another in the 4–0 victory for an FA team against the RAF at Tottenham. He did all the scoring in a victory at Brentford, made a three-goal switch to centre forward in the absence of the injured Lambden in a 5–1 away win at Notts County and earned a 3–3 draw at Luton a few days before again starring, but not scoring, as the FA defeated the Army 3–1 at Newcastle.

Against Brentford on 5 September an outstanding piece of work by Meyer, 15 minutes before half time, gave Bradford his first goal. Moving out to the right wing, Meyer fooled left-back Frank Latimer, and when he floated the ball across the goal, Bradford, unmarked, headed it in. A minute after the start of the second half a move between Meyer and Watling finished with the winger sending across a perfect centre. Again Bradford met the ball with his head, placing it into the corner of the goal, well out of goalkeeper Reg Newton's reach. Just 15 minutes from the end, Petherbridge finished one of the many fascinating runs with a pass that Bradford only had to push over the goal line. Following a draw and two successive defeats towards the end of September, the recent 'goal-shy' mood of the forwards was worrying Bert Tann, who tried the surprise experiment of playing Bradford at centre forward against Southampton reserves at Eastville on Monday 21 September. With a forward line comprising Biggs, Roost, Bradford, Meyer and Bush it came as no surprise when the visitors were defeated 5–0 with Bradford notching another hat-trick. After 37 minutes a good Watkins clearance sent Bush away, and Bradford guided his low, hard centre behind goalkeeper Fred Kiernan and into the net. Steeds made a fourth goal for Rovers in 57 minutes when he beat three defenders, held off all challenges, and then flicked the ball through for Bradford to score with a right-footed shot which again left Kiernan helpless. Bradford got his third in 67 minutes when he shook off two defenders and banged a hard shot into the net, this time with his left foot.

Five days later at Notts County, Bradford began a run of seven games at centre forward, having previously made only one senior appearance in that position, in his inaugural season with Rovers. Bradford leading the league attack then proceeded to take three opportunities brilliantly to get yet another hat-trick. The first came from a grand piece of work by Petherbridge that made Rovers' second goal 7 minutes before half time and gave Bradford his opener. The Rovers winger screwed the ball low across the Notts County goal and Bradford pivoted round to beat Gordon Bradley with a lightning shot. His second came when he fired past Bradley following a grand move by Bryan Bush, and Bradford obtained his hat-trick with an amazing goal in the 70th minute. Bradley, troubled by an awkward bouncing ball, dribbled it down the wing before clearing, but it was returned by Fox for Bradford to hit the ball first time in to an empty net. Against Luton on 31 October Rovers

...and the Hat Trick

Here they are—the three goals by Geoff Bradford which brought promotion to Eastville. In the pictures at the top and on the right Bradford is down on the turf as the ball reaches the net. Above: He gets a close-up of his first goal.

Three-Goal Bradford was in Pain for 90 Minutes

Rovers' final home match saw them defeat Newport County with a Bradford hat-trick on 25 April 1953 to secure promotion, with two matches still to complete at Aldershot and Crystal Palace.

went ahead after 23 minutes. From a Bryan Bush centre Bradford got his head to the ball and deflected it out of goalkeeper Bernard Streten's reach. In the 62nd minute Bradford beat one defender in a tackle, raced between two more, and unleashed a shot from 25 yards which left the goalkeeper helpless as it rocketed into the net. About 6 minutes from time he completed his first first-team hat-trick at Eastville of the season. Bradford got his head to a bouncing centre from Bush, got it under control and swept it with his right foot all along the ground past Streten's diving body. With twenty goals to his name and the season only just over two months old, Bradford was at the height of his career, firmly in line for elevation to an England place. Quite what Rovers might have achieved if he had remained injury-free remains a moot point, for a career-threatening leg injury, suffered after he had scored the opening goal at Plymouth Argyle in November, was to rule him out for almost six months.

4

REPRESENTATIVE HONOURS AND FULL ENGLAND DEBUT

Geoff's goalscoring reputation continued to flourish and this brought him to the attention of the Football Association selectors and more importantly the England selectors. Towards the end of only his third season as a professional, Bradford won his first representative honour when selected to play for a Football Combination XI against a Paris XI in the French capital on 20 March 1952. The London Combination/Football Combination representative sides tended to be a mix of genuine reserve players and temporarily 'demoted' senior players from clubs in that competition. However, at the time of his selection neither of these criteria applied to Rovers' leading scorer who finished the 1951/52 season making 45 league appearances and scoring 26 goals. There seems to have been the usual Anglocentric double standards of the time at work: YOU put up your best, WE'LL put up a selection from a-long-way-down-our-pecking-order, and we'll obviously beat you. But, just in case, we'll bolster our boys with one or two related 'ringers'. Indeed for the annual Paris match the Combination selectors included Alf Ramsey of Tottenham Hotspur at right-back, who had won some 30 full England caps at the time. Selected at inside left, Bradford, always an accurate marksman with chances in front of goal, made no mistake with his first chance in a representative game. Following a scrappy opening, the Combination attacked and after 2 minutes Bradford scored with a cross shot and then went close with another effort, heading a Les Medley centre against the bar. The other Third Division man, Maurice Owen of Swindon, scored 5 minutes from the end as the match finished in a 2–0 victory to the visitors.

Selection for a Football Association XI followed in October 1953 when Bradford, who was given the distinction of captaining the youthful team, scored a hat-trick in a 4–0 win over the Royal Air Force at White Hart Lane. His hat-trick was his fifth in senior football that season and brought his tally of goals in senior football to 100 in a little over three seasons. Right from the start, when he won the toss, he showed the value of direct methods, racing out to the left to force a corner in the first minute. After half an hour came his first goal, when Derek Hines zipped out to the right and passed to the centre, where Bradford was waiting to crack a terrific 15-yard shot which was blocked by Jeff Hall on the line. But Bradford followed up with great speed and a second shot from 6 yards gave no-one any chance to save. Three minutes later came goal number 99. A lob from the left bounced awkwardly for him, but Geoff raced up, got a foot to it and lifted it high and then, with perfect coolness, nodded it over Wood's head into the net. The goal which notched up the century and completed the hat-trick after 70 minutes was one of Bradford's best, according to *Bristol Evening World* reporter Pat Kavanagh. In a run parallel with the goal he beat Ron Flowers and Bryan Edwards, deceived Harry Webster into covering an expected pass to the right wing and then, on the turn, unleashed a terrific 25-yard drive which gave goalkeeper Ray Wood no chance as it speed just inside the top corner. Among the thin crowd there was a pause, a gasp, and then a roar of applause to greet the best goal seen on the Spurs ground that season – and the FA selectors, sitting in the directors' box, were looking thoughtful. Bradford got no more goals in the second half but he created three more sitters for fellow forwards which they missed. And towards the end he made another gilt-edged chance for himself, but this time decided to be unselfish and tried unsuccessfully to put the ball on a plate for Hines. 'A pity that, because in international stuff you take the goals when they are

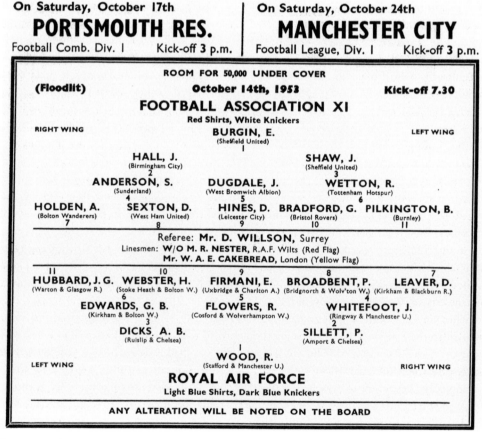

Programme for the FA representative match on 14 October 1953 against the RAF played at Tottenham Hotspur. Bradford captained the FA XI and scored a hat-trick in a 4–0 victory.

there,' wrote Kavanagh, 'An England "B" cap looks a certainty now, and if that goes well and his club form keeps to its present standard full honours seem just around the corner.' In the match Dave Sexton of West Ham added a fourth goal for the FA.

It is worth pointing out the calibre of the opposition who, although representing the Royal Air Force, were all young professional footballers who were doing their stint of compulsory National Service. The RAF team included the likes of Ron Flowers of Wolves, Ray Wood of Manchester United and Alan Dicks and Peter Sillett, both of Chelsea. Bradford, as one of the professional players selected by the FA, was allowed travelling expenses and a fee of £6, but while shorts, stockings and numbered shirts were provided by the Football Association, players were requested to bring their own soap and towels!

On the train journey from Paddington back to Bristol Temple Meads Bradford was witness to the subterfuge to which Rovers had resorted to sign Norman Sykes as a professional for the club. Sykes, who had captained Bristol Boys, played for England schoolboys and had won a place in the England Youth team, was being pursued by a number of clubs. Bert Hoyle was enlisted to take the sixteen-year-old Sykes to stay with the former Rovers goalkeeper's relatives in Bradford for a week. The day before his seventeenth birthday, Sykes and Hoyle travelled from Yorkshire to London, to join up with Bert Tann and Bradford, who were there for that match in which Bradford scored three of the FA team's four goals in the defeat of an RAF side. On the train, the four men checked their watches, and one minute before midnight Tann produced the forms that Sykes signed to become a Rovers professional.

Bradford's next representative match was in the north-east at St James's Park, Newcastle, on 4 November that same year, once more selected for the Football Association in a game against the Army. Although designated an FA XI it was considered by the FA selectors as an England 'B' side. In a mediocre match it was local hero Jackie Milburn who brightened up the evening with two goals in a 3–1 win. However, any hope of Bradford winning a first England cap was shattered at Plymouth on 7 November 1953 when after scoring Rovers' third goal against Argyle he received a serious injury to his right leg which put him out of the game for six months. As well as depriving Rovers of their ace goalscorer the injury stalled Bradford's progress of receiving further representative honours and the possibility of full international recognition.

On the Wednesday before the Plymouth game he had played for the FA XI against the Army at St James' Park, Newcastle, and was due to travel to Belgium on Monday 9 November as he had been selected to play for the Football Combination against the Brussels League on the Wednesday night. While the Football Combination was drawing 2–2 in one of the stormiest matches played by an English side in Belgium, Bradford was recuperating from his injured leg in a Clifton nursing home. He made good progress in recovering from the career-threatening injury, sufficiently so to be selected for the final league game of the season on 24 April against Stoke City, when in front of a rapturous crowd he scored a hat-trick as Rovers won 3–1. Despite having played only one league game since the previous November, Bradford was named by England Director of Coaching Walter Winterbottom in the England party being considered for the 1954 World Cup finals in Switzerland. The news that Bradford was on the 'shortlist' was received at the Eastville club on 26 May, but it was kept secret, although Bradford was informed. His response, in his usual modest manner, on hearing the news, was: 'That's wonderful!'

Geoff visited Ireland with Rovers in the summer of 1954. He is pictured kissing the Blarney Stone.

After returning from Ireland with the Rovers party, Bradford had recommenced training and finished it on the Sunday, the day before he left Bristol on the morning of Monday 31 May to join the other England players at the Star and Garter Hotel, Richmond. The twenty-five squad members assembled for three days' training at the Bank of England Sports Club's ground, Roehampton. The group included legendary England internationals Billy Wright, Tom Finney, Tommy Taylor, Jimmy Dickinson and Nat Lofthouse. Stanley Matthews, then nearly 40, and Tom Finney were not involved in the training; Matthews had asked for a rest following a tour of the Continent with his club, Blackpool, and Finney was having treatment for a thigh injury. Winterbottom was in attendance during the get-together, but it was Alan Brown, the former Burnley and Notts County centre-half, out in the middle in charge of training. Practice matches were arranged between Whites and Reds following training sessions with, on one of the days, Bradford coming on as a second-half substitute for the Reds, replacing Fulham's Johnny Haynes, who defeated the Whites 4–2. He was played for 20 minutes in one practice match and half an hour in another, selected in both as an inside right, but when Jimmy Mullen was hurt in the second game, he took the winger's place at outside left.

Bradford played in these matches without his injured knee bandaged and he did not feel any reaction. Jimmy Trotter, England's trainer, had had a look at the injury when the players first met. Bradford was told before he left the training camp that he had given a good impression with his play, despite the fact that he was never played at centre forward, which was his best position and the one he liked to operate in. Peter Barnes considered that Bradford, in international class, was a centre forward or nothing, as he did not have the ball craft to play in top-class company as an inside forward. 'He was selected in the first place because of his amazing goalscoring ability. And to me it is beyond understanding why he was not tried where the goals are expected to come from – at centre forward. Nat Lofthouse and Bedford Jezzard were the two centre forwards that week. Bradford proved himself the most dangerous player in front of goal in the country last season, and he never did better than when in the middle,' commented the *Evening World* reporter. The final squad selection was submitted to FIFA on 8 June and it would have been too much to expect a place for Bradford in the seventeen-man squad which travelled to Switzerland for the tournament or to be chosen as one of the five reserves who remained at home awaiting a call if the need arose, but it was testament to Geoff's determination and powers of recovery that following his setback and lay-off he was still considered to be one of the top twenty-five English footballers of the day. Had Bradford been chosen for England, his sensational return after being out of the game for five and a half months to win his first cap would have been the most astounding comeback in soccer history. Bradford had naturally hoped to top-off his comeback by winning a trip to Switzerland, but even he considered it too much to expect. 'My leg would not stand the strain of overwork, and I lacked speed,' he said. Neither did he subscribe to the common view that he would have stood a better chance of going with the chosen seventeen to Switzerland if he had come from a more fashionable club. 'But that's a lot of hooey. The fact is this time I wasn't considered good enough. I'm hoping there will be a next time. It's largely up to me,' he informed a reporter at the time.

Eager to resume his stalled career following the enforced lay-off and summer break, Bradford got off to a flying start in the 1954/55 season, carrying on from where he had left off in a frenzy of goalscoring. He scored the only goal against Port Vale and was to score 19 goals in 14 league games by 23 October, scoring in every one of Rovers' first six games. Ten of the club's dozen goals in that period were credited to him. Ultimately, he was easily the club's top scorer with 26 Second Division goals. In the first week of September, he scored two hat-tricks in 48 hours, first in a 4–1 home victory over Derby County and secondly as Liverpool were defeated 3–0 at Eastville. The goals against Derby came in a frantic 18-minute spell in the opening half hour, with Peter Hooper adding the first of his many Rovers goals. After 9 minutes Bradford beat Frank Upton and Colin Bell and then sent in a hard, low shot which left goalkeeper George Hunter standing. It also beat Roy Patrick, standing on the line. Bradford got his second when Hooper chipped the ball into the middle. The pass left him clear and he had plenty of time in which to tee the ball up before sending in a terrific rising shot which rattled into the net off the upright. Only 2 minutes later the hat-trick was complete. After Paddy Hale and Bill Roost had made the running, Bradford rounded centre-half Ken Oliver, took the ball out to his left and then sent a left-footed shot well out of Hunter's reach. The Liverpool game was the seventh in succession in which Bradford had scored, a new club record which was to last just eighteen months. In the 42nd minute Bradford sent in a glorious header, from a Petherbridge centre, well out of Liverpool 'keeper David Underwood's reach. A minute later, from just inside his own half, Bradford raced fully 35 yards downfield, body-swerving his way past three defenders en route, and then crossed out to the right before cracking in a terrific shot which Underwood reached but couldn't stop. The crowd cheered Bradford off the field at half time, and they had every right to – he had scored two great goals. On 87 minutes he completed his hat-trick, albeit a little fortuitously. Hale had a shot handled and blocked by a defender, but the ball ran through to Bradford who, standing offside, had been played on by the Liverpool man. This presented Bradford with the easiest of chances and before Underwood could look round the ball was bulging the back of the net. At this stage, in fact, Bradford had scored in each of his last nine league appearances if his final games before injury in November 1953 are taken into consideration. As a postscript, Rovers set off for Devon where the 1954/55 season was rounded off by an extraordinary friendly, won 10–6 at Dawlish, with Bradford contributing four of the goals.

Talk of an England cap for Bradford was at its height after the international selectors had seen him score a hat-trick in the 3–0 demolition of Liverpool on 6 September 1954, and it certainly seemed a little closer when he was named as a reserve for the Football League's match with the Football League of Ireland at Dalymount Park in Dublin on 22 September. Fate, however, favoured the other reserve, Johnny Wheeler of Bolton Wanderers, who impressed in a 6–0 victory, while Bradford's hopes of an England call receded when he failed to score as Rovers conceded five goals in both their next two games at West Ham and Liverpool. Another chance to impress the selectors presented itself at Ashton Gate on 22 March 1955 when Bradford was picked again for the Football Association in a match against the Western League, with the FA secretary Sir Stanley Rous among the crowd who watched the 3–0 victory.

Opposing Bradford in the Western League side under the floodlights were Eastville team-mates Barry Watkins and Alfie Biggs, but it was Bradford who raised a cheer among Rovers fans that night. A second goal for the FA XI came after a Mike Tiddy centre, low and hard, came into the middle. Two shots were kicked off the line before the ball came out to Bradford, who promptly hooked it into the net from close range. Before half time a header from Bradford struck the crossbar. The dull play of the second half was enlivened 15 minutes from the end by a fantastic effort by Bradford, who scooped the ball over the bar from a couple of yards' range to the astonishment of the 4,278 crowd, and no doubt a few friendly jeers from the City fans present.

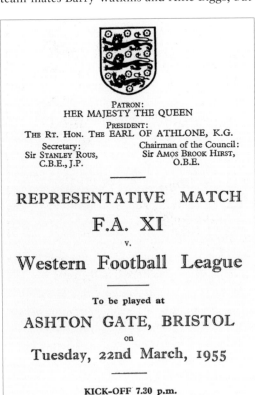

PATRON:
HER MAJESTY THE QUEEN
PRESIDENT:
THE RT. HON. THE EARL OF ATHLONE, K.G.

Secretary: Chairman of the Council:
Sir STANLEY ROUS,   Sir AMOS BROOK HIRST,
C.B.E., J.P.   O.B.E.

REPRESENTATIVE MATCH

F.A. XI

v.

Western Football League

To be played at

ASHTON GATE, BRISTOL

on

Tuesday, 22nd March, 1955

KICK-OFF 7.30 p.m.

Bradford was selected for another FA representative match, this one against the Western Football League in Bristol on 22 March 1955. Rovers team-mate George Petherbridge was a reserve for the game.

GEOFF WAS BORN ON 18TH JULY 1927 AT BRISTOL. THIS 6 FT. FORWARD JOINED BRISTOL ROVERS IN 1949–50, AND HAS SCORED (UP TO FEB. 26TH 1955) 133 GOALS IN 210 FIRST TEAM APPEARANCES. THIS GOAL SCORING MACHINE REGISTERED 5 HAT TRICKS IN THE 2ND DIVISION AND ONE FOR THE F.A. vs THE R.A.F. DURING THE 1953–54 SEASON; TWO HAT TRICKS IN ONE WEEK THIS PAST SEASON AND WAS SKIPPER OF THE F.A. XI vs THE R.A.F. AT WHITE HART LANE IN 1953, THE F.A. XI VS THE ARMY AT NEWCASTLE IN 1953, THE FOOTBALL COMBINATION XI. vs PARIS (IN PARIS) IN 1952. HE HAS REPRESENTED ONLY ONE PROFESSIONAL CLUB, THE BRISTOL ROVERS WHOM HE HAS SERVED IN ALL THREE FORWARD POSITIONS.

Geoff BRADFORD

HU SEALY.

A superb caricature of Bradford, by Trinidadian cartoonist Hu Sealy, which was included in a local souvenir brochure published for the 1955 FA tour of the West Indies.

Bradford was selected for the English FA tour to the West Indies in 1955, and was accompanied in the party by seventeen players, fifteen fellow professionals and two amateur players. It was a reciprocal visit as the Trinidad FA had visited England in 1953, when a Trinidad team had played Bristol Rovers in a friendly match at Eastville during their tour. The FA selectors had considered a remarkable number of players for the six-week tour including: 14 goalkeepers, 39 full-backs, 66 half-backs and 97 forwards before finalising their tour squad. The party consisted of: goalkeepers Ted Bennett (Watford) and Harry Sharratt (Bishop Auckland); full-backs Grenville Hair (Leeds United), John Hall (Birmingham) and Jimmy Langley (Brighton); half-backs Tony Emery (Lincoln City), Peter Goring (Arsenal), Jimmy Hill (Fulham), John Kelly (Blackpool) and captain Syd Owen (Luton); and forwards Geoff Bradford (Bristol Rovers), Vic Groves (Leyton Orient), Ron Heckman (Bromley), John Hoskins (Southampton), Bedford Jezzard and Bobby Robson (both Fulham), Gordon Nutt (Cardiff City) and Stan Pearson (Bury).

The party assembled under the managership of Joe Richards and his trainer/coach Harry Wright at Lancaster Court in central London on Monday 9 May 1955, flying out that evening to Bermuda. Prior to the party's departure the West Indian press was devoting many column inches to the forthcoming tour and Geoff Bradford in particular. On 9 May the *Jamaica Gleaner* had this to say about the Rovers star striker:

Geoff Bradford may be at inside-right or centre-forward on the English FA team which plays here at Sabina Park on Wednesday night, May 18, Saturday night May 21 and Monday, May 23. Not even his Bristol Rovers manager, Bert Tann, knows his best position. But wherever Geoff plays he will be among the goals, they are his specialty, especially hat-tricks. Last season he notched five. And for six of the nine-month season he was laid up with a serious knee injury. He returned for the last match for the season and scored three goals against Stoke. This proved his fitness and earned him a place in England's party that went to Switzerland last year for the World Cup. This season he is again Rovers' top scorer. Geoff was married in 1951. He had a 24-hour honeymoon before reporting back to soccer training.

The tour started on 12 May with a match against Bermuda played in a temperature of 80°F on the Prospect Garrison Field, Hamilton. Bedford Jezzard astounded the home side with his powerful shooting, scoring four goals, while Bradford contributed two goals in an emphatic 11–1 victory.

A much-changed Bermuda side, now designated a Bermuda FA XI, were hammered 14–1 in the following match despite the home goalkeeper performing heroics. Both goals conceded by the FA team to Bermuda in the opening two games were own goals – netted by Owen and Langley respectively. The FA squad then moved on to Jamaica arriving in Kingston where the touring party were well received with much hospitality and sightseeing. In the first of the three evening games at Sabina Park against Jamaica in five days the tourists ran out 7–0 victors twice and in a more competitive second match won 4–2. The two home goals in the second game on the island were greeted with great delight from the crowd. Bradford scored in all the three matches and netted two superb hat-tricks. In the opening

The FA team who played against Bermuda on 12 May 1955. Back row, left to right: Harry Wright (trainer), Frank Adams (FA), Geoff Bradford, John Kelly, Ted Bennett, Peter Goring, Syd Collings (FA). Front row: Vic Groves, Jeff Hall, Jim Langley, Joe Richards (FA), Syd Owen, Bedford Jezzard, Bobby Robson, Johnny Hoskins.

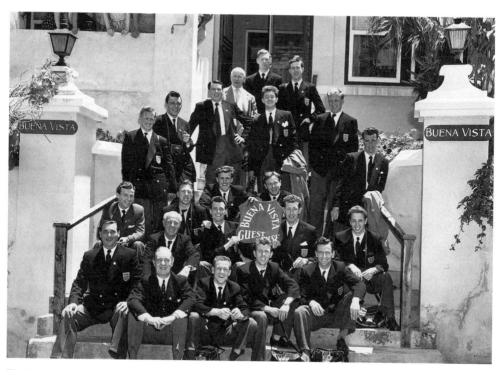

The FA squad pictured outside of the Buena Vista Hotel, in Paget Parish, south of Hamilton Harbour, where the tour party stayed during their visit to Bermuda. Geoff is in the front row far right.

game on 18 May, the first ever played under floodlights in Jamaica, a Groves to Jezzard to Bradford triangular movement in the 35th minute ended with Bradford directing a bumping ball over the crouched shoulder of Kenny Williams for the final goal of the first half.

'Hat-Trick Bradford Did It Again Last Monday Night', ran the headline in the *Jamaica Gleaner* on 25 May. 'The scheming Bristol Rovers inside forward tallied his usual quota of three as Jamaica, for the second time in the "300" Tercentenary soccer series, bowed out 7–0 to the touring English FA XI at Sabina Park,' reported Baz Freckleton, following the third Jamaican match of the tour. After 13 minutes the first goal came when Bradford, soaring to meet a corner kick from outside left Johnny Hoskins, headed the ball down into the bottom corner of the northern goal. A corner was conceded on the right during an FA attack and the resultant corner kick from outside right Vic Groves reached Bradford's head just outside goalkeeper Henry Miller's reach to enter the net in the 30th minute for the second goal. Bradford completed his hat-trick in the 73rd minute when he dribbled around Miller and tapped past Williams who was completely fooled by a late bodyswerve.

A short flight to Trinidad followed where all the matches on the island were played at Trinidadian cricket grounds – three of which being at the Queen's Park Oval, Port of Spain, and the other at San Fernando. The first against North Trinidad was by far the

most difficult of the tour. The only goal came from Jezzard just 8 minutes from time. A record crowd of 16,000 watched the next match but a remarkable display from the tourists saw them rattle in six goals without reply. Bradford scored twice in the first game against Trinidad in the 6–0 victory and scored a first-minute goal in the next game at Skinner's Park, San Fernando, where he bagged another hat-trick in the 8–1 win. A further two-hour flight to the Dutch colony of Curaçao and the final two matches of the tour followed on 7 and 10 June at Willemstad where both games were drawn, with Bradford playing and scoring in the penultimate tour match which ended in a 2–2 draw.

Bradford, centre, and two FA team-mates take a break during a sight-seeing visit on the tour of the West Indies.

The touring party also had the opportunity to watch the third day's play of the Fifth Test in Kingston between the West Indies and Australia on their way home following the conclusion of the successful tour. The eleven-match tour which lasted six weeks resulted in nine wins and two draws, 69 goals were scored and just 8 conceded by the tourists. Bradford was joint top scorer along with Bedford Jezzard of Fulham, with 15 goals apiece; Bradford's total included three hat-tricks. The tour forged good long-term friendships – Geoff Bradford and Bobby Robson, both future full England internationals, kept in touch throughout their respective careers and in retirement. Robson went on to successfully manage Ipswich Town and Newcastle United, coached clubs in Spain, Portugal and Holland, and managed the England national team. As well as the West Indies being geographically another world, the temporary lifestyle of the English players and officials while in the Caribbean was in many respects a very different world to the one normally inhabited by the Rovers man who lived in the shadow of the Eastville gasworks. As a professional player Bradford received a weekly allowance of £15 per week during the tour. A daily allowance was paid to the amateur players.

Given a £50 allowance prior to the commencement of the tour, for the purchase of lightweight clothing, the FA supplied a comprehensive list of attire required on the trip to attend the various functions. Parties were given for the tourists at the Hamilton Armoury and St George Dinghy Club in Bermuda, they attended receptions, resplendent in blue blazers and grey flannels, with the governors of the islands they visited, as well as numerous cocktail parties, banquets, lunches, picnics and dances. While in the Caribbean Bradford was introduced to the delights of rum, which plays a great part in the culture of most islands of the West Indies, and brought some bottles home for his family and Rovers team-mates. Geoff experienced the excitement of Arima Horse Race Club, boat trips, sea bathing and a visit to the Sergeant's Mess of the Duke of Cornwall's Light Infantry in Jamaica. Watching Australia bat against the West Indies in the Fifth Test at Sabina Park, Bradford and his team-mates lunched with both sets of players, which included such well-known West Indian cricketers as Clyde Walcott, Everton Weekes, Frank Worrell, Garfield Sobers and Ray Lindwall, Keith Miller, Neil Harvey and Richie Benaud of Australia.

The goalscoring feats of Geoff Bradford clearly came to the attention of the England selectors. He received a call-up and the details of his selection for the Full International against Denmark in Copenhagen on Sunday 2 October 1955 were posted to him by the Football Association.

The selection card Geoff and his family cherished gives full details of the itinerary, such as: 'all players to assemble at Lancaster Court Hotel by 1.00 p.m. on Friday 30 September for motor coach transport to London airport at 2.30 p.m. Flight BE 220A departs for Copenhagen 1620 arrive 1840 hours. Players will stay in the Hafnia Hotel.'

After the match they would be dinner guests of the Danish Football Association. On Monday 3 October they were due to depart Copenhagen airport flight BE 221A at 1635 hours to arrive at London airport at 1820 hours. Fees and expenses were to be paid to and from London plus £2 per day during the period spent abroad. The playing fee was £50. After his England appearance Bradford bought a new full-length coat and a second-hand

PATRON:
HER MAJESTY THE QUEEN
PRESIDENT:
H.R.H. THE DUKE OF EDINBURGH, K.G., K.T.

Secretary: Chairman of Council:
SIR STANLEY ROUS,   A. DREWRY, C.B.E., J.P.
C.B.E., J.P.

International Match

Denmark v England

To be played at

COPENHAGEN, DENMARK

on

SUNDAY, 23rd OCTOBER, 1955

Kick-off 1.30 p.m.

The front cover of the FA selection card Geoff received for his full England international debut against Denmark in Copenhagen on 2 October 1955. The incorrect date was printed on the card!

The England team for the match with Denmark played a practice match behind closed doors against Charlton Athletic. Left to right: Ron Baynham, Jeff Hall, Roger Byrne, Bill McGarry, Joe Kennedy, Jimmy Dickinson, Jackie Milburn, Don Revie, Nat Lofthouse, Geoff Bradford, Tom Finney. Captain Billy Wright was unavailable for the warm up match so Kennedy of West Bromwich Albion stood in for him.

The England team assembled at Lancaster Court Hotel, London, prior to the match with Denmark. Left to right: Roger Byrne, Nat Lofthouse, Jackie Milburn, Don Revie, Jeff Hall, Geoff Bradford, Stan Anderson (reserve), Bill McGarry, Tom Finney, Ron Baynham, Jimmy Dickinson, Billy Wright.

car with the money earned from his match fee. Not many footballers owned cars in those days, but Rovers team-mate George Petherbridge was one of the first to get a vehicle to travel up from his Somerset home to Bristol.

Bradford became the first, and still the only, Rovers player to make a full England appearance while with the club. The Bristol Rovers Supporters' Club committee, chaired by Eric Godfrey, decided that they wanted to watch Geoff's England debut and made arrangements to charter an aircraft to fly from Whitchurch Airport in Bristol to Copenhagen. Getting hold of match tickets was a concern as the FA said only 100 were available for the whole of the country's supporters. Rovers Secretary John Gummow informed the FA of the club's plans to charter a flight, requesting them to apply to the Danish FA for additional tickets. The supporters' club even offered to pay the cost of any necessary telephone calls. Eventually 34 tickets were forthcoming, but the committee then had the difficulty of sorting out who travelled, as there were more applications than seats on the Dakota aircraft supplied by Cambrian Airlines.

Bill Creed, the supporters' club honorary travel secretary who made all the arrangements, was accompanied on the trip by Geoff's wife, Betty, an invited guest of the supporters' club. Others in the Rovers party included Ron Batt, who became a longstanding committee member, George Fouracre, John Gummow, Rovers' Secretary, John Coe of the *Bristol Evening Post* and Pat Kavanagh of the *Bristol Evening World*.

Members of Bristol Rovers Supporters' Club, with Mrs Betty Bradford as their guest, flew from Whitchurch Airport, Bristol, on Sunday 2 October 1955 to Copenhagen to watch Geoff's England debut. Betty is on the left of the group of three ladies.

THE FOOTBALL ASSOCIATION BULLETIN

November 1955   One Shilling

The front cover of *The Football Association Bulletin*, dated November 1955, illustrates England captain Billy Wright leading out his team in Copenhagen. Bradford is the seventh player in the line.

After setting off from Whitchurch the aircraft landed at Blackbushe Aerodrome in Camberley for refuelling before continuing its journey to Copenhagen. On arrival the excited group of Rovers supporters were taken by coach to the Idrætsparken Stadium by which time the match was already in progress. The massed bands of the Coldstream Guards, Black Watch and Gordon Highlanders played before the kick-off and at half time, and the teams presented to King Frederick of Denmark, who attended with Queen Ingrid, both being very interested spectators among the record crowd of 53,000. The game was played to inaugurate the new main stand at Idrætsparken.

The headline in the *Times Weekly Review* read 'Undistinguished Victory' as the match proved to be a straightforward England win. However, it all made for a momentous occasion, and Bradford rose to it by scoring once, making goals for Lofthouse, and having one controversially disallowed, which saw Bradford race away and slam the ball past the advancing Henriksen – but the linesman's flag was up for offside.

The original plan was for Bradford to play up front with Lofthouse, and for Don Revie, the other inside forward to operate in midfield. In the event, however, Revie was the one to play up front and Bradford was left to do the fetching and carrying. Don Revie opened the scoring after 26 mins with a penalty, after Finney was brought down by Olesen as he prepared to shoot. On 33 minutes Henriksen, under pressure in the air, dropped an awkward lob into the penalty area from Jeff Hall and when Bradford's quick shot rebounded off Lofthouse, the Bolton centre forward was on hand to dribble and drive home from close range. Just before half time came the best goal of the match to send England 3–0 up, a position they scarcely deserved. Receiving from Billy Wright, Bill McGarry in midfield sent Bradford away on a long run down the left. As the low centre flew in, Finney cleverly feinted and let the ball run on free to the unmarked Lofthouse straight in front of goal. There was only one end to that.

The opening half had been a mixture of lethargy and glimpses of skill. What came after was an anti-climax in spite of a few bits of artistry. The man to supply them, the man who tried to make England play in attack, was Revie. Wright, too, recovering from a stuttering start never put a foot wrong in the last hour as was his way and in Dickinson he had an experienced lieutenant in defence. But it was Revie, the architect, who caught the eye and brought pleasure with his positional play, execution and general sense of design. After many misses in the second half, England at least did extract two well cut goals.

Soon after the change of ends, Revie shot in a flick from Milburn splendidly on the run from 15 yards to add England's fourth and his second goal of the match. At 10 minutes from full time, Bradford rounded things off as he ran onto a long forward pass from Milburn which spilt the Danish defence. The ball came to him awkwardly, but he brought it under control, evaded a tackle by Jensen, and slammed the ball with his right foot along the ground past goalkeeper Henriksen into the net.

In between England's second-half goals the Danish crowd was excited for a short while when Lundberg headed past Baynham for their only goal after 62 minutes, but the Danish captain and his colleagues had long since lost any authority, in spite of the efforts of Jensen and Olesen at wing-half. Just 4 minutes from the end Bradford was injured in a heavy, two-footed and illegal tackle by left-back Nielsen and was attended on the field by trainer

Geoff Bradford holds off a strong challenge to score England's fifth and final goal in an emphatic 5–1 victory watched by a record crowd of 53,000.

Jimmy Trotter. Fortunately the right leg was only jarred, and although Bradford was winded when Nielsen fell on top of him during the incident he was soon back on his feet and in play again. One Rovers fan recalled a voice in the crowd shouting 'Come on, Soundwell!' a reference to Bradford's first club.

When interviewed following his international debut the modest-as-ever Geoff revealed to the two Bristol newspaper journalists that he had, 'Done alright, I hope so anyway,' as Mrs Bradford confided she was 'wildly happy' when her husband scored and 'was in the main stand and had a wonderful view of everything – I did not jump up and clap – I never do.' While England manager Walter Winterbottom was quite satisfied, 'although we missed many chances particularly in the second half,' he mused, his opposite number was more forthcoming remarking, 'We had no complaints,' adding, 'Billy Wright and Geoff Bradford were England's best players.' Yet one of the London reporters opined that 'with plenty of space in which to work he [Bradford] did a few good things, but did not impress as an international inside forward.' It was at least conceded that 'he took his goal well'. Rovers fans and football supporters generally could judge for themselves as 12 minutes of recorded highlights of the match were shown on BBC television the following night at 10.45 p.m., with Kenneth Wolstenholme commentating on the game. Despite England's biggest win abroad since the 10–0 pulverising of Portugal in Lisbon in 1947 failing to attract wholehearted praise from the critics, Bradford and his England colleagues were praised by manager Walter Winterbottom after the match and advised they would all keep their places for the game against Wales the following month. However, in a private moment before he left the dressing room Bradford was taken aside by Winterbottom to say the England selectors wanted Johnny Haynes for Geoff's position in the Welsh game. In those days the selectors chose the England side, not the manager, and they had picked the side to play against Wales before the Denmark game had been played. Winterbottom was quite upset

Bradford wearing his treasured England cap and jersey.

about the situation, 'but not so much as I was,' recalled Bradford in 1992. Geoff was understandably distraught after being on such a high from his debut, scoring a goal and playing well and then collectively advised they were all to play against Wales. His hopes were shattered. Privately he remarked it was the most disappointing moment of his entire career.

His chances of being called up again by his country had been blighted because, when commenting years later, in his opinion, 'the London football reporters were determined to get the young Johnny Haynes into the England team instead of me,' adding, 'I'm sure that in those days what the national press said had a considerable bearing on who was selected for the England team. I'm not disputing for one moment that Haynes was a great player, but I'm convinced that if selection had been purely on merit I would have kept my place after the Denmark game.' It was suggested in some of the newspapers that it would be a better team if Haynes was playing, but it was neither Haynes nor Bradford who filled the inside left position in Cardiff, as Dennis Wilshaw of Wolves was recalled for the 2–1 defeat at Ninian Park. But it was not only Haynes who kept Bradford of unfashionable Bristol Rovers out of the team. The Rovers marksman's age (he was only a few months from his 28th birthday when he was capped) also counted against him – as did the fact that, in addition there were a good number of other, and younger, players putting forward strong claims. Among these was John Atyeo, Bradford's corresponding 'big gun' on the Bristol football scene over at Ashton Gate.

Just ten days after his full international debut on Wednesday 12 October, undaunted, Bradford played for the Football Association in a challenge match against the Royal Air Force. The game was played at Bristol City's Ashton Gate ground and drew a crowd of 23,396, and proved to be a showpiece for Geoff's good friend and Bristol City forward John Atyeo to display his magnificent talents. Although the opposition was overrun almost from the start, Atyeo's strength, speed, enthusiasm and shooting power was something to behold, as the brilliant play of the local hero contributed four of the nine goals by the FA past a luckless Gerry Cakebread. Bradford opened the scoring on 10 minutes, with Atyeo adding a second, a penalty, after 20 minutes.

The game was far too one-sided to merit it as a competitive encounter although the RAF's Ray Parry, an inside forward, and winger Brian Pilkington, both contributed clever touches.

PATRON:
HER MAJESTY THE QUEEN

PRESIDENT:
H.R.H. THE DUKE OF EDINBURGH, K.G., K.T.

Secretary: Chairman of Council:
SIR STANLEY ROUS,   A. DREWRY, C.B.E., J.P.
C.B.E., J.P.

Representative Match

F.A. XI v Royal Air Force

To be played at

ASHTON GATE, BRISTOL

on

WEDNESDAY, 12th OCTOBER
1955

Kick-off 7.30 p.m.

Ten days after his full international debut Bradford played at Ashton Gate for the FA against the Royal Air Force watched by 23,396 spectators. He scored twice in a 9–0 hammering with Bristol City's John Atyeo impressing with four splendid goals.

Bristol City's John Atyeo was a good friend of Bradford. At 5 years and 161 days younger than Geoff he scored 315 goals in 598 league appearances for the Robins. Atyeo made his England debut against Spain just eight weeks after Bradford had made his international debut and he scored too. Atyeo scored five goals for England while winning six caps.

The power of the FA forward line enabled the spectators to see some brilliant top-speed goals and powerful shooting. Vic Groves on 30 minutes and another Bradford goal after 43 minutes ensured a 4–0 interval lead. Second-half goals and a hat-trick from Atyeo on 67, 77 and 85 minutes, with Bedford Jezzard netting two goals after 70 and 75 minutes, completed the rout. Bradford had opened the scoring after 10 minutes. Played on after he trapped a 25-yard shot by Barnes which was going wide, he crashed the ball into the roof of the net, beating Cakebread in a fraction of a second with disarming ease, but expert efficiency. His second goal came after Jack Boxley made a good run and centred to Bedford Jezzard, whose shot was only partially cleared. Out came the ball to Bradford and he slammed in an explosive shot which struck a defender's head as it rocketed in.

A few minutes after the final whistle Walter Winterbottom selected his squad for the England 'B' international fixture against Yugoslavia at Maine Road. It contained three full internationals. Bradford was one of three reserves. 'We had been led to understand,' said Bradford, 'that the same side would be chosen for the "B" match with Yugoslavia a week later at Maine Road, but before I left the ground I was told by Walter Winterbottom, the England manager, that Haynes had been chosen to play against Yugoslavia before the RAF game, and that I would be twelfth man. I had scored two goals against the RAF, and laid on at least three more, but again my performance counted for nothing.'

Bradford was again overlooked when the national selectors had a rethink for the match in which Northern Ireland were defeated 3–0 at Wembley on 2 November, neither could room be found for him in the Football League side that won 4–2 against the Scottish League at Hillsborough, nor in the England team that enjoyed a 5–1 romp against Yugoslavia in a 'B' international. He was not even in the FA XI that drew with the Army at Newcastle, and there was no room for Bradford among the seventeen players called up for special training before the game with Spain at Wembley at the end of November, as younger men were ahead of him in the queue, regardless of the fact that around this time he was in tremendous goalscoring form. Disappointingly there would be no second chance for Bradford with England.

Selected again for the Football Combination, Bradford's final representative game was against a Dutch National XI on 24 October 1956 in Amsterdam where he contributed two goals (19th and 76th minutes) in a resounding 6–0 victory, in front of 30,000 spectators, over a Dutch side that had only a few changes from the national side that had beaten West Germany, the World Cup holders, two weeks earlier. According to one newspaper report, there were 'at least ten offside decisions against Bradford in the second half, most of them hairline,' and although he put the ball in the net a third time the effort was disallowed.

5

TWO CAREER-THREATENING INJURIES

Geoff Bradford's story of high achievement is all the more remarkable for the fact that he twice had to battle back from a serious injury that would have forced less resolute players into retirement. The first of the injuries came at Plymouth Argyle on 7 November 1953, at a time when he was strongly in line for an England cap. He had been told to stand by for the England party preparing for the 1954 World Cup in Switzerland for which England had qualified by winning the 1953/54 British Home Championship. Bradford had already scored five hat-tricks that season, four in the league, one of them for an FA side against the RAF at White Hart Lane in October. Another three goals had come in the 5–0 Football Combination match against Southampton at Eastville on 21 September. The inclusion of Bradford in the reserve side provides an indication of the type of man he was as, although the club star at the time, he volunteered to play for the reserves because the side was short of players and the first team had no game. Bert Tann thanked him, put him in and watched him grab yet another hat-trick.

Bradford had just taken his league goals tally to 18 in Rovers' 17th game of the 1953/54 season, giving them a 3–2 lead early in the second half at Home Park, when he chased a pass from George Petherbridge down the right wing. As he centered the ball he slid down with his right leg stretched out, and Paddy Ratcliffe, the Pilgrims' left-back, came down on that while tearing across to make a late challenge. The leg was numbed, the bottom part of it out at an angle from the top half, but Bradford managed to crawl over the touchline as trainer Bert Williams went to help him. The female surgeon at the Plymouth hospital to which he was taken for X-rays wanted to keep him there, but Bert Tann insisted that he went straight back to a private nursing home in Bristol, so the leg was strapped up and Bradford returned on the team coach. Bradford recalled afterwards that he considered that the manager's decision not only saved his career, adding, 'If it had not been made I might never have walked properly again.' The orthopaedic specialist who operated on his damaged leg at the Chesterfield Nursing Home in Clifton found that that the heavy tackle had chipped the top of the fibula bone, severely damaged a cartilage, which he removed, and torn away a ligament at the knee joint. The decision to operate so quickly was taken by the specialist after Bradford had been placed under an anaesthetic to allow a thorough examination of the damaged right knee. If the severed ligaments had been left any longer they would have shrunk back and it might have proved impossible to join them again. He was given the news

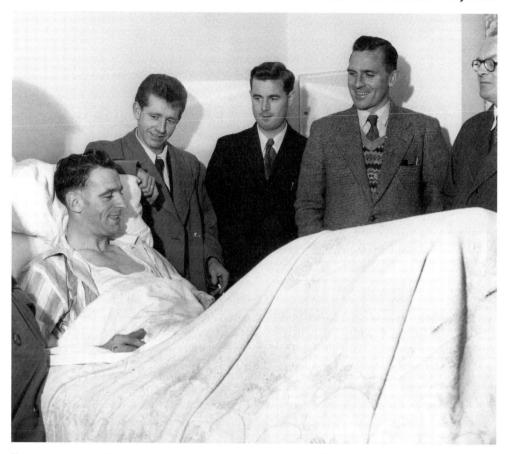

Team-mates Bryan Bush, Peter Sampson and Vic Lambden visit Geoff in hospital while recovering from the injury he sustained at Plymouth Argyle.

by a specialist after the orthopaedic operation on the right knee that as a result of the injury he would not play again until, at the soonest, Christmas.

Although he wasn't informed at the time, the experts considered it probable that Bradford would never kick a ball again. For Bradford the injury was a double blow, as it meant that he missed the Football Combination representative midweek game in Brussels, but even more important – it took away the strong chance he had of being awarded an English international cap that season, as he had already been seriously considered for the inside left position against Northern Ireland on 11 November at Goodison Park. It was a grave blow, too, to the Rovers, who would badly miss the man who had already that season scored 24 goals, 21 in senior football. Bert Tann, whose telephone rang incessantly as football fans wanted to know how the man who had scored six hat-tricks during the season was, spent most of the day at the nursing home on the Sunday. Geoff, he said, was bright and cheerful. 'I'll be all right, boss,' he had assured Mr Tann. 'It's a pity I'm going to be out of the game for so long, but it could have been worse.'

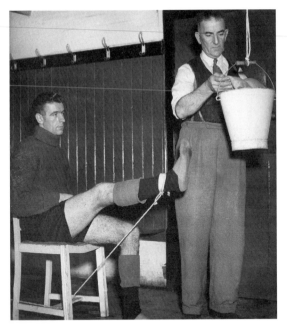

Rovers' trainer Bert Williams devised a bucket and weight system to assist Bradford to recover from his first knee injury. Geoff had scored 18 goals in the first 17 matches of the Pirates' first season in the Second Division then missed 24 games due to injury. Remarkably he scored a memorable hat-trick in his comeback in the final match of that season against Stoke City.

Bradford was in the nursing home for two weeks following the operation to repair his right knee, and then on crutches for six weeks with a full-length plaster cast on the leg. Once the size of the plaster cast had been reduced, he began to go to Eastville for exercises on a stationary bicycle under the supervision of trainer Bert Williams. His initial treatment at the ground consisted of heat-ray therapy and massage of both legs to get the muscles back into trim. Flexing his right knee and occasionally putting his weight on it began the process of rehabilitation which was stepped up as time went on. It was Williams who devised a pulley system that allowed the injured striker to lift buckets of sand with the injured leg.

He was still using crutches in between exercises but once they were thrown aside in January, Bradford began walking around the Eastville pitch perimeter. Progress was good as planned and by the end of the month, with his legs almost ready for full training, trotting around the pitch commenced. When he wasn't on the treatment table and to help fill in the long hours between the exercise sessions, he sat in the club office helping secretary John Gummow with the mail and any other job he could lay his hands on. He was happy making his twice-daily trips to Eastville Stadium for his little exercise and his chat with the rest of his colleagues. Geoff did not talk a lot himself, but he was content to listen to the banter which went on between the rest of the boys, and if he needed an incentive to return he was able to have a look at his 'strips' hanging on the peg. The final stage in bringing Rovers' star striker back to full fitness was as described by Bert Tann 'geeing up' to fully stretch the muscles which had not been used for so long, testing the power of the right leg. Manager Tann was not prepared to put Bradford back into the hurly-burly of league football until he was completely satisfied that he was fit and ready, and if necessary he would be given the whole of the remainder of the season and the close season to get himself back to the hat-trick form he had shown before the injury.

This routine continued, with Bradford slowly regaining fitness, until April and the final week of the season, at the beginning of which he persuaded the reluctant Bert Tann to let him play in a Thursday evening Football Combination game. A record reserve team gate for Bristol of 13,542 gave Bradford a great welcome at Eastville against Brentford Reserves, the club managed by Bill Dodgin Senior, when he played his first match since his injury at Plymouth on 7 November. They cheered him as he ran on and off the field and every time he kicked the ball. Geoff responded by scoring both goals in a 2–1 win which gave Rovers a valuable brace of points in their struggle to reach Division One of the Football Combination. Everyone was waiting for that first goal of his which came in the 8th minute of the match. Before, he had tried a left-footed shot which just missed an upright and one with his right foot which was diverted by a defender for a corner. Then Watling and Roost opened up an attack on the left and when the winger centred, there was Bradford. But he had to withstand a heavy tackle by two defenders before he could ram the ball into the net. What a cheer went up! Bradford showed class in everything he did. Despite the awkwardly bouncing ball he could still beat his man and his distribution, the long pass out to the wing or the side-footed flick through, was the best thing in what was always an entertaining match. Bradford, with a heavily bandaged right leg, hooked another into the net only to be ruled offside before his second goal on 38 minutes. This time the opening was made on the right by Lambden and McIlvenny and when the winger crossed low, Bradford moved into the right place at the right time to steer the ball past goalkeeper Alf Jefferies. Afterwards

Bristol Rovers' first team, 1953/54. Back row, left to right: Bert Tann (manager), Jackie Pitt, Harry Bamford, Howard Radford, Geoff Fox, Peter Sampson, Bert Williams (trainer). Front row: George Petherbridge, Paddy Hale, Geoff Bradford, Barrie Meyer, Peter Hooper, Ray Warren.

Rovers manager Bert Tann said, 'He did everything I wanted him to do after a long lay-off.' In an article penned by Bradford some time later, he wrote about his comeback, 'Two days previously I had turned out for the reserves in my first match for months. You can imagine I felt pretty jittery as I went on to the field, wondering if everything was going to come out all right. As it happened, I got a couple of goals and felt fine.' The following morning, Bradford pestered Tann to select him for the first team for their final Second Division match of the season on Saturday 24 April 1954, at home to Stoke City. Rovers were in tenth place in their first season in Division Two with the Potters two places below, so neither team were involved in promotion or relegation matters. The manager agreed, but with such trepidation that he went off to watch Rovers reserves at Southampton on the match day, saying that he 'couldn't bear to watch'. It was the first match he had missed since taking over from Brough Fletcher in January 1950.

What he missed was something out of the wilder realms of schoolboy fiction as Rovers won 3–2 and each of their three goals was scored by Bradford, the hat-trick expert. Recalling the tremendous cheers from the crowd that erupted as the match-winning goal went in, Geoff years later said, 'If I had to pick out one moment as meaning more to me than any other, then it would be that one.' The game he remembered was the one which gave him confidence to carry on with his career after an injury which would have finished many lesser players for good. It is a game which will also be remembered by everyone who was there, and it was a remarkable attendance – almost 23,000. There was a big enough cheer when his first goal went in from a Petherbridge centre after 40 minutes. It rose to a crescendo when a great header brought a second, and the third which completed his hat-trick had the crowd on its feet, shouting, waving and, many of them, weeping. Lambden's centre, after 77 minutes, seemed a shade too fast and too near the goalkeeper to constitute a real menace, but Bradford, displaying his old form, flung himself forward in the air, timing his effort to a split second and was in an almost horizontal position when he headed the ball into the net past goalkeeper Bill Robertson. It was a superb piece of opportunism, and within a minute it was followed by the match-winner. Hooper put over an accurate centre and Bradford outjumped the Stoke centre-half to nod the ball into the net again well wide of the goalkeeper. 'I have never seen any player get a greater ovation than Geoff Bradford did as his header soared into the net in the 78th minute to complete his hat-trick,' wrote *Evening Post* reporter John Coe. There is not much room for sentiment in football, but it was felt right from the start of the game that the crowd, almost to a man, were behind Geoff Bradford in his effort to stage a comeback. And how nobly he responded to their vocal encouragement, as on half a dozen occasions he tore through the Stoke defence. Rattles, scarves, hats went high in the air, and as one man the people in the stand rose to their feet to cheer. Bradford had had many fine moments in the past, but never one more triumphant than this. It was a comeback which many people said couldn't happen. But his determination, mental and physical, had given the lie to any thought that injury, serious though it was, could write off a career just as it was promising international recognition. When congratulated as he was leaving the field, Bradford, in his usual modest manner, merely said, 'It was a little hot out there.' To Geoff most matches were alike – just another game – but even this undemonstrative player agreed

Geoff heading past Rovers goalkeeper Howard Radford during a training session at Eastville.

that there was something special about it. He had yet to find completely the old speed and judgement, but after all he had been out of the game for most of the season.

Bert Tann paid high tribute to the skill with which trainer Bert Williams treated Bradford's knee when he started to come down to the ground after leaving hospital. 'But of course,' he said, 'Bradford owes his recovery to himself more than anybody for he alone had to bear the pain. His determination was amazing and I shall never forget watching him on the cycle machine when his injured knee would not bend. He would jam down with his other foot to force his knee to give, and I have seen him leave that machine on a cold winter's day with the perspiration rolling down his face.' At the completion of the league programme, Tann announced that Bradford would be having his first benefit during the coming season.

Rovers' players, manager Tann and trainers Bert Williams and Wally McArthur formed a party of thirty-four that went under canvas at a Weston-super-Mare training camp just before the start of the 1954/55 season. Tann thought that it might help to have all his players together for 24 hours a day for a fortnight in an innovative experiment to bond his squad. At the beginning of August the group assembled at the Uphill Road Sports Ground where there was a fine marquee as a dormitory, alongside elephant huts which were used as a dining hall and dressing rooms. One hut was used as a cookhouse, where a gas stove was installed. On the evening a *Western Daily Press* reporter visited the location, it was a scene of great activity, 'Three players were taking their turn at potato peeling, others playing cricket with a makeshift wicket and a few were having golf practice.' The camp was within 200 yards of the beach, affording facilities for sea bathing, and the site formed part of the Weston golf links. There were three football pitches available. Local youngsters were invited to free coaching sessions, conducted by a dozen senior professionals under the direction of Bert Tann, and young holidaymakers, too, were invited. Youths from several local clubs took part in the sessions, and on the Tuesday evening those leaving work dashed up on motorcycles and bicycles already changed until the pitch was swarming with tutors and pupils, all having practice in ball control.

Rovers' camp broke up from Saturday 7 until Monday 10 August, and then continued until the following Saturday with daily spells of training. Once the season had started, after initial incredulity and scorn, Rovers were contacted by clubs from all divisions of the Football League asking for details of what went on at Weston. They wanted to know the schedules of training, how the players liked them and what effect they had had on the standard of play in league matches. Even more importantly, they were asking if and how the intensified schedules were being continued while the season was in progress. Some even asked if they could visit Bristol and watch Rovers in training. Tann had introduced his new ideas as a pure experiment and however much he may have felt hurt at the derision of the unbelievers early on, he was completely cooperative, and within reason other clubs who wanted information or a 'look-see' at the stiff training sessions were allowed in.

Back at Eastville the pre-season public trial on 16 August saw the Blues triumph 6–2 over the Reds with Bradford scoring a hat-trick, in a match played over 50 minutes each way. He scored his first two goals by merely applying the finishing touch to skilfully engineered movements by George Petherbridge. But the best of the three was his third, when he volleyed a pass from Petherbridge into the net before goalkeeper Chandler had time to move. Bradford, having fought his way back to full fitness and his good form and goalscoring prowess undiminished by the enforced lay-off, scored 26 league goals, notwithstanding a missed penalty against Ipswich Town on 9 April, in the following campaign as Rovers finished in 9th place, and had notched a further 26 in 28 league and cup appearances in the 1955/56 season when he suffered an almost identical injury to the other leg. Rovers had achieved a famous victory over First Division Manchester United with Bradford scoring one of the goals in the 4–0 third round FA Cup win on 7 January, providing them with a fourth round tie with Doncaster Rovers at Eastville.

The third round of the FA Cup on 7 January 1956 produced what is arguably the best ever win by a Rovers team in history, as the 'Busby Babes' were taken to the cleaners in a superb performance in front of just under 36,000 fans at Eastville. 'BIGGS AND Co. CANE "BABES" 4–0' ran the headline to the match report, by Pat Kavanagh of the *Pink 'Un*, which read as follows:

> Manchester United – the famous 'Busby Babes', leaders by four points in the First Division – were pulverised by Rovers at their cup-fighting best. Alfie Biggs scored two great goals, while Barrie Meyer netted and Geoff Bradford successfully took a

penalty. Only goalkeeper Ray Wood saved the United from a heavier defeat, and this victory must rank as the best in the Eastville club's history. Before a full house in this all-ticket match, the captains, Pitt and Byrne, received a great cheer from the crowd as they led their teams onto the field. There was a special one for Ron Nicholls, the Rovers goalkeeper who, in the absence of Radford through injury, was making his cup debut. United were missing England international star Duncan Edwards. The pitch, still heavy, was generously sanded, particularly in the centre of the field. Pitt won the toss and the Rovers, facing the Arches end, but with no apparent advantage from wind or sun, were soon on the attack through Sampson and Bradford, but Jones kicked back to Wood for relief as Biggs tried to race through. Pitt found Petherbridge with a perfect pass but the winger's pass went astray and once again Jones passed back to Wood just wide of Bradford as the Rovers leader raced in. Bamford had two clever clearances on the right and then Sampson and Bradford sent Petherbridge away, but the winger's centre dropped onto the top netting. Pegg and Taylor tried to get the United line moving on the left, but their passing was too short, as Doherty joined in, and Hale cleared. There was a certain amount of miskicking before Violett sent Taylor away on the right flank and Nicholls dived to save a waist-high shot from the United leader. Almost immediately, there were two thrills in the United goal area. First, Hooper got the ball into the middle, and Bradford's first time shot went wide, and then Wood had to move backwards to block the ball as Hooper breasted towards the line a Petherbridge centre after a perfect opening by Biggs. Biggs played really well in the opening stages and made another opening from which Wood dived to Bradford's feet to force the Rovers man to shoot wide of the near upright from close in. The easiest chance so far came when Doherty moved over to the left, crossed the ball, and Berry's centre caught the defence napping. It dropped right onto Violett's head, but although unmarked, he headed the ball two yards wide. It was a bad miss, and the United were to pay dearly for it, for in the very next minute, the Rovers were ahead. Meyer made the opening in midfield, and his centre came off a defender to Biggs, whose quick, right-footed shot beat Wood completely as it curled inside the upright.

The Rovers came again and Byrne was hurt in a collision with Biggs, as Bradford tried to head a Petherbridge centre home, but he resumed after treatment. Biggs forced another corner after a free kick against Jones, but this was headed away by the tall centre-half. The United had two free kicks and for the second, against Pitt, Byrne lifted the ball into the goalmouth, where it was safely collected by Nicholls. Straight away Hooper sent a perfect through-pass to Meyer, who beat two men on the run before sending a high rising shot from 20 yards a foot over the bar. The Rovers seemed to be tackling much harder than usual although it was fair, and three times in succession Allcock stopped the lively Berry. Biggs on this day looked as good as any of the United stars, and with his aid Bradford moved to right and left to make openings. Allcock conceded United's first corner after Pegg had taken advantage of a free kick quickly taken by Byrne and a second followed, and from this the ball rolled to the feet of Berry, whose angled shot beat Nicholls, but was a foot wide of the far post. Manchester attacked strongly, moving the ball with delightful skill, and when Pegg tried to slip the ball across to the waiting Taylor, Nicholls collected it at the foot of the post. Byrne conceded another corner to Petherbridge after Jones had been penalised for pushing Bradford, but this was headed away although the United goalkeeper had another escape when Wood palmed away a centre from Pitt. Hooper promptly flicked the ball into the middle and Biggs tried a remarkable overhead shot. With the keeper well out of position, the ball went inches over the bar. Another Rovers corner was fought off before Berry put United on the attack and Bamford was penalised on the fringe for obstructing Pegg. It was Pegg who took the kick and promptly sent the ball wide of the line-up into the net, but it was no goal because the free kick was indirect and the ball had not touched any other player. Nicholls saved an awkward shot from Pegg although it was a second attempt. Only a desperate 'Rugby' tackle from Jones brought down Bradford as he broke into the clear with a pass from Pitt. After Nicholls had deflected a Taylor shot which looked as though it might have been going in, Jones was booed by the crowd for the way in which he blocked Bradford. Biggs was penalised for obstructing Wood. A few minutes later, Jones was spoken to sternly by the referee when he brought down Petherbridge. From this corner, Biggs jumped high to Hooper's kick, and his header beat Wood completely, but was kicked off the line by Byrne. Bradford was hurt in a goalmouth scramble as he went up with Jones for a high cross, but he resumed after treatment. A quick shot by Pegg went square across the face of the goal to the far corner flag before Allcock was able to clear. Hooper and Bradford raced through on the left for Biggs to head the winger's centre into the side netting. Thirty seconds before half time, Petherbridge made the opening from which the Rovers increased their margin to two. His centre went straight to Meyer, whose first shot was blocked, but the ball came back to the inside right, and he made no mistake with his second attempt from six yards.

Half time – BRISTOL ROVERS 2–0 MANCHESTER UTD

There was a scramble in the United goalmouth as Hooper burst through. Woods moved quickly as Bradford tried to flick it goalwards. Pitt cleared well as Taylor tried to force his way through. For a while, the United defence was under heavy pressure and after Biggs had a storming shot charged down by a defender, Bradford forced Jones to concede a corner. Three times in quick succession, Hooper weaved his way past the puzzled Foulkes, but on the last two occasions he found no-one in support. Nicholls made two brilliant stops when he collected a header from Colman beneath the bar, and then punched away the centre from Pegg when Taylor seemed certain to score. Hale conceded a corner from Taylor as Violett schemed an opening, but Doherty headed wide of the upright. As the Rovers came away, Hooper, played clear by Petherbridge's long pass, sent in a shot which beat Wood, but slid wide of the far upright. Pitt was wide with a shot from the edge of the penalty area. Meyer had another blocked and a third from Petherbridge cannoned off Byrne and away for a corner.

Bradford is on hand to watch Alfie Biggs' second goal, and Rovers' third, fly past Manchester United goalkeeper Ray Wood in the FA Cup third round tie on 7 January 1956.

The United captain had to receive treatment from the trainer before Wood held Bradford's header from just beneath the bar. A long cross from Bradford, who had chased a clearance from Allcock, led to a third goal by the Rovers in 62 minutes. It went straight to Petherbridge, who flicked the ball inside to Biggs, and the young Rovers forward, steadying himself, beat Wood completely, with a low shot from 15 yards.

The United forced a corner immediately afterwards, but this was badly placed by Pegg. As Meyer moved into an open space on the right, Wood made a brilliant stop as he dived to Bradford's feet. Wood had to knock down a hard centre from Petherbridge meant for Bradford. Biggs almost scored a third as he beat two defenders, and sent in a scorching shot from 20 yards. Wood jumped frantically to punch the shot over the bar. Again Wood was beaten by a Bradford header but the ball skimmed the crossbar. Wood brought off another wonder save from Biggs as he palmed the ball away for a corner. Another header from Bradford missed by inches. For almost half an hour, it had been practically all Rovers. Wood brought off another great save from Hooper, and two more from Bradford and Petherbridge. Hooper had another shot saved by Wood and Byrne headed off the line a shot from Meyer. Immediately afterwards the Rovers were four up after a Bradford header had been punched out by Byrne. Bradford took the penalty, and as the ball sailed into the net, the strains of 'Goodnight Irene' rang out over the ground. 'Byrne had seen me take a penalty before,' Bradford recalled, 'and he went up to tell Ray Wood, United's goalkeeper, which side of the goal I was going to place the ball. Ray said: "I know where he's going to put it; it's a question of whether I can get there in time." And as the ball sailed past his dive into the back of the net, his question was answered.'

Bristol Rovers: Nicholls; Bamford, Allcock; Pitt, Hale, Sampson; Petherbridge, Biggs, Bradford, Meyer, Hooper. Manchester United: Wood; Foulkes, Byrne; Colman, Jones, Whitefoot; Berry, Doherty, Taylor, Violett, Pegg. Referee: Mr Ken Aston, Ilford. Attendance: 35,872.

United gained revenge some years later when they defeated Rovers 4–1 at Old Trafford in January 1964 with Denis Law scoring a hat-trick despite a remarkable performance by Rovers' goalkeeper Bernard Hall. Geoff remarked that the splendid performance by Law was the best individual display by any footballer he had ever seen against him. Law won European Footballer of the Year that season.

A hat-trick by Bradford against Hull City on 21 January emphasised the good form he was in that season, which was to end prematurely for him in the fourth round FA Cup replay at Doncaster on the last day of January. Played under floodlights on an extremely cold Tuesday night, Rovers had outplayed the Yorkshire side the previous Saturday, but Eddie McMorran had equalised Peter Hooper's penalty. There was uncertainty as to whether Bradford would play in the replay, as he had taken a knock during the first game. There was doubt about his fitness and Bert Tann had thought of keeping Bradford back for the league match the following Saturday as Rovers were going well in the Second Division.

Bill Roost was standing by as a replacement, but the Rovers manager made a late decision to include Bradford in the side. The FA had agreed to floodlights being used from the third round of the FA Cup, following their use in a recent England International which saved the game from being abandoned in deteriorating conditions, so the replay became

A superb example of Geoff Bradford's heading power in a match against Nottingham Forest at Eastville.

the first competitive match to be played under lights at Doncaster's ground. It very nearly also became the first to be televised from there, but when the FA gave permission for the second half to be screened, the home club flatly refused the BBC approach, only to reconsider when compensation for loss of gate money was offered. However, the amount of the compensation was then not thought sufficient, and after a day of frenzied negotiations the BBC reluctantly announced that they had been unable to come to terms 'in time for the necessary technical arrangements to be made.' Bristol Rovers played well on the frozen, snow-covered Belle Vue pitch, but failed to take their chances, and were then rarely out of their own half after the interval. Alfie Biggs had the ball in the net in the 28th minute but was given offside and 2 minutes later Bradford had a shot from 30 yards just held, and then head-flicked inches wide of an open goal. With 20 minutes of normal time left and the score sheet still blank, Bradford challenged for the ball with two Doncaster defenders as Paddy Hale drove a free kick upfield. This was how Geoff recalled what happened next: 'As I put my left leg up to control the ball one Doncaster player Charlie Williams [later a well-known stand-up comedian] moved in on one side of me, and another defender on the other. They blocked my leg between them. It was a pure accident, not even a foul, so play continued as I went down on the frozen snow. It was just over two years earlier that I had last felt pain like that. In my heart I think I knew then it was a similar injury, but I dragged myself to the touchline and Bert Williams and the Doncaster trainer helped me to the dressing room. As I lay there I heard the home cheers greeting the late goal that brought Doncaster victory.'

Bradford was put to bed at the Rovers' hotel after being strapped up by Doncaster's club doctor. The following day, the problem was how to transport Bradford to the railway station for the return to Bristol, but that was solved by the provision of a wheelchair on which he was taken to the train. 'I arrived there in what you might call a state, but that was where the VIP treatment ended,' as he recalled the difficulties of the journey home. 'They wanted to put me in the goods van, but I didn't fancy that idea, so they managed to prop me up along one of the carriage seats.' Back in Bristol, he was taken home before returning to the Chesterfield Nursing Home because he wanted see his wife Betty first. Operated on that same night the surgeon identified that the two main ligaments in the

Geoff enjoyed playing lawn tennis for many years at the Civil Service Sports Club, Horfield and Cleeve Hill Tennis Club, Downend.

News of Bradford's selection for England ensured warm congratulations from his Rovers team-mates. Captain Ray Warren shakes his hand watched by, from left to right, Alfie Biggs, Jackie Pitt, Ian Muir and Harry Bamford.

left knee this time had snapped, and both cartilages had gone. The only difference to his previous injury was that there was no cracking of the bone. Two days after the operation, propped up in a hospital bed, Bradford thought that he had a touch of indigestion, as he explained: 'Something seemed to be lodged in the left side of my chest, so I asked Betty to massage it for me, and rang for the nurse. I asked Betty to give it another good rub and as she did I could feel something move across my chest. I began to get short of breath, and by the time help arrived a lung had collapsed. At that point I lost consciousness.' The doctors diagnosed that a clot of blood had moved up from the left leg and gone into the lung and for the next few days Bradford was confined to an oxygen tent, with nobody allowed to see him while he remained on the danger list. His treatment continued without the comfort of his loved ones, he recalled: 'I was given a series of injections to break up the clot, and after a couple of days Betty was able to see me. They said that the clot was probably the result of the amount of ether that had had to give me during the three-hour operation. I could taste ether for days afterwards and for five or six days the leg injury took second place to the collapsed lung.' Bradford remained in hospital for just over two weeks and in plaster once again for a further six weeks, although on 3 March Rovers made arrangements for him to be transported to Eastville to see his club play against their old rivals Bristol City in the league.

To help him regain complete fitness after his second knee operation Bradford took up lawn tennis and showed that a natural ball player can excel in any sport. Bradford had been selected to go on the FA's two-month tour of South Africa and Rhodesia in the summer of 1956, but he had not recovered from his second serious injury sufficiently by May when the eighteen-man party which included team-mate George Petherbridge and Rovers' coach Fred Ford departed for Africa.

6

COMEBACK AND THE QUEST FOR FIRST DIVISION FOOTBALL

In the history of any football club there is a key moment where fate can determine success or otherwise. In the case of Bristol Rovers, bereft of their injured talisman, Geoff Bradford, two late defeats at the end of the 1955/56 season meant missing out narrowly on promotion to Division One. The role of Bradford in the Rovers story cannot be underestimated as he scored in all but four of his first seventeen matches of the season, seven times scoring twice in a game. Potentially key games at Stoke City and Hull City early in 1955 were both won 2–1, Bradford scoring the goals on both occasions.

Then, having scored a hat-trick in the return fixture with Hull City on 21 January, Bradford was seriously injured in the FA Cup game at Doncaster Rovers ten days later. The Hull side included the veteran Stan Mortensen, scorer of a hat-trick in the 1953 'Matthews' FA Cup final and the holder of 25 England caps, but it was Bradford who stole the show with three goals. He got a fine goal 3 minutes after the interval to place Rovers within reach of Hull who were two goals ahead at half time. The move started with Biggs and Petherbridge on the right and as the winger sent his cross towards the far post, the Rovers leader threw himself forward and headed the ball in from close range well out of Bill Bly's reach. Pitt, who had been playing so well, made the opening from which Bradford scored another great goal after 50 minutes to put Rovers level. Pitt's pass went to Hooper and as the winger lobbed the ball into the middle, Bradford outjumped the defence to score with a fine header. Just 2 minutes from the end Bradford completed his hat-trick when he turned on a pass from Hooper about 10 yards out. Bly quickly advanced to narrow the angle but the Rovers centre forward slammed the ball with his left foot well out of his reach, to finish off a fine 4–2 win.

When a Bradford-less Rovers lost at Blackburn in the next match after the FA Cup replay at Doncaster, the Pirates dropped to sixth place in the division, but soon recovered their form and three successive victories at the beginning of March elevated them to second position as the season drew towards its conclusion. The fixture at Elland Road on 21 April 1956 was one of the more crucial league matches in Rovers' history. With Sheffield Wednesday virtually champions, Rovers lay second with 48 points and two games remaining with a real possibility of promotion to the top flight for the first time in their history. Leeds United,

Bradford tries a shot during an Eastville game watched by Paddy Hale and Bill Roost (9).

Geoff (on bicycle) shares a joke with his team-mates at one of Rovers' Weston-super-Mare summer training camps. From left to right, standing: Peter Sampson, Bill Roost, Jackie Pitt, Ray Warren, Josser Watling. Sitting: Jimmy Anderson, Ian Muir, Alfie Biggs.

with three games left, had 46 points, one more than Blackburn Rovers and Nottingham Forest. Victory for Rovers at Leeds would leave the Eastville side requiring a point at home to Liverpool for promotion to Division One and in eager anticipation the supporters' club once again chartered an aeroplane for the trip north. Dai Ward had scored crucial goals in recent weeks and his goal after 2 minutes at Elland Road set a club record, as it was the eighth consecutive league game in which he had scored, eclipsing Bradford's seven in succession earlier in the season, which had equalled his own record achieved in 1954. Before half time, though, John Charles had headed home a George Meek cross and set up Jack Overfield for what proved to be Leeds United's winning goal. The Elland Road crowd, 49,274, remains the largest league crowd before which Rovers have played. So Bristol Rovers went into the final Saturday unhappily aware that their hopes of joining the league's elite had gone, with supporters complaining that the opportunity had been missed because no experienced centre forward had been signed to take the place of the injured Bradford. Their goal average was inferior not only to Leeds United's, but also to those of the three other clubs with whom they were to finish four points behind the Yorkshire club. Once the bubble had burst, on the final day of the season Rovers also lost to Liverpool 2–1, in front of 24,000 home fans. Sheffield Wednesday were champions with 55 points, Leeds United promoted with 52, while Liverpool, Blackburn Rovers and Leicester City all inched above Rovers on goal average. So close to their target, Rovers fans were left to wonder what might have happened if 25-goal top scorer Bradford had not been injured and why no adequate replacement was found. A final placing of sixth in Division Two remains the highest in Bristol Rovers' history.

Every day during the summer of 1956 Bradford went down to Eastville and trained on his own. As the new season approached he went to Rovers' training camp at Weston-super-Mare with its special beach training and brine baths and was not spared, playing in both private and public practice games. In the evenings he played lawn tennis.

With the whole of the summer to ensure that his recovery was complete, there was naturally great interest among the fans in Bradford's appearance in Rovers' pre-season public trial match held on Monday 13 August 1956. A remarkable attendance of 8,080 went to Eastville Stadium that night with one object in view – they wanted to see Geoff Bradford score a goal, but they were disappointed even though his team, the Blues, won the match. But the crowd was not disappointed in his performance as his distribution delighted those present, and Bradford who led the Probables first team attack, made three of his side's nine goals, distributed some delightful passes over long distances, and positioned himself well – but no goals for centre forward Geoff. Still without any doubts he proved his fitness and hit some powerful shots with both feet, especially in the hard and fast first half in which what appeared to be the league side was pitted against the reserves. 'I felt a bit strange at first but I had been a long time off football and I expected it. Still it was fine to be back. I have suffered no ill-effects and am quite satisfied with my fitness,' said Bradford after the match, which resulted in a 9–3 victory for the Blues over the Reds. 'And what's more. He never hesitated in the tackle,' the *Daily Mirror* encouragingly reported. 'It feels great to be back, and my first league game can't come soon enough. I'm perfectly fit now,' reported Bradford after coming through the public trial match that clubs used to hold at the time.

Geoff Bradford during a pre-season training session at Eastville in July 1956.

Manager Bert Tann and his players watch film coverage of one of their matches to enable tactics to be discussed and performances improved.

On 18 August Bradford, the new Rovers captain, led out Bert Tann's home-grown side, which had come so close to an unlikely promotion to Division One the previous season, for the opening fixture of the 1956/57 season against Grimsby Town. However, his return to league action did not bring an immediate re-establishment of his previous good form, as the *Evening World* reported, 'Bradford was the big query in the game, and it remains a question mark. We must wait for a while to discover whether the old dynamic Geoff Bradford, whose spectacular goals swept him into the England side last season, is to return to league football. Only once in the game did he get up to send through a typical Bradford header, and although he missed narrowly with two well-placed ground shots there was little power behind either. And that long, raking stride which used to carry him through opposing defences was missing as well.' Ever supportive of his star striker, Bert Tann came to Bradford's defence. 'Let's be fair to him. He has been out of match play since last January and that's a very long time,' said the Rovers chief. 'Physically he is quite fit, but after two serious injuries in three seasons he is bound to be a bit cautious at first. It will take him four or five weeks to play himself back to his top form.'

By the following Thursday evening for the game at Leyton Orient it appeared that he was almost back to the Bradford of a season ago, as he played really well in the 1–1 draw. Bradford didn't score but shirked nothing and brought a number of fine saves from goalkeeper Pat Welton and caused the Orient defence no end of trouble. Despite being selected for the first six league games at the start of the season and scoring five goals as Rovers won four of those opening games, Bradford admitted that he was 'never quite the same player I had been before. I had lost my quickness in turning and hitting the ball, and that had been my strength.' There was therefore no real prospect of his adding to the one England cap he had been awarded against Denmark, less than a year before. Rovers scored in each of the first fourteen league games of the new season to complete a run of 24 consecutive matches dating back to March 1956. Two more games would have equalled a club record established in 1927, but Rotherham United held Rovers to a goalless draw at Millmoor in October.

Geoff relaxes from the strains of professional football by playing a game of bar billiards at the Eastville Club in Bristol.

The early season run included a 4–2 win at Doncaster Rovers, Bradford scoring twice, and a 4–0 home win over Stoke City, as Rovers remained unbeaten in their opening five league fixtures. Bradford began 1957 by scoring two of the goals in a 4–3 win at Hull that earned Rovers a cup visit from Preston North End, but that was Rovers' only success in five matches before his exclusion from the goalless Eastville clash with Bristol City on 2 February. Alfie Biggs was switched to centre forward, and the vacancy on the other side of him from Dai Ward's repositioning was filled by Norman Sykes. Bradford had been dropped from the Rovers attack 'to be groomed as a back', reported the *Daily Express* on 23 February. Bert Tann, perhaps having second thoughts as to whether or not Bradford would regain his old form announced, 'I've long thought that of Bradford making a fine back,' and told him, 'You can come back against Barnsley – at left-back.' In fact it was as centre-half that Bradford returned to the side against the Yorkshiremen in February, followed by a second game at the centre of the defence, before a move to right-back versus Rotherham on 9 March. The short-lived move to defensive duties ended after only three games and Bradford was reinstated to the forward line for the final seven matches. While not maintaining the previous season's results during the 1956/57 campaign, a modest return for Bradford, of 11 goals in 25 league appearances, helped sustain Rovers' quest for First Division football until the final month of the season, when a ninth place finish was still creditable.

The *West of England Football Annual 1957–1958*, published at the start of the season, gives an interesting insight into how the local football world viewed Bradford's performances post-injury. 'Bradford himself was enigmatic. Caught by injuries on the one hand and psychological reservations on the other, he was seldom at his best, but Mr Tann has sufficient faith in Geoff's powers of recovery to believe the 1957/58 season will herald a return of that match-winning form that so excited the club's supporters three years ago.' Indeed, when discussing Bradford it is always well to remember that a lesser player would have given in to the injuries he had been cursed with, long long before.

The FA Cup is a tournament filled with excitement and expectation, although in Rovers' case early disappointment is all too frequent an occurrence. In 1957/58, for the second time in the club's history, however,

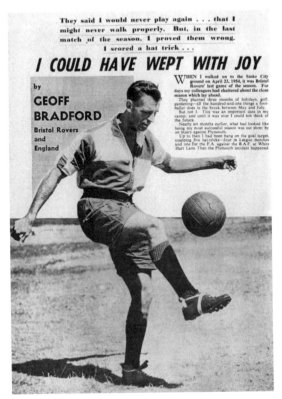

Bradford had an article about his career published in a 1956 football annual.

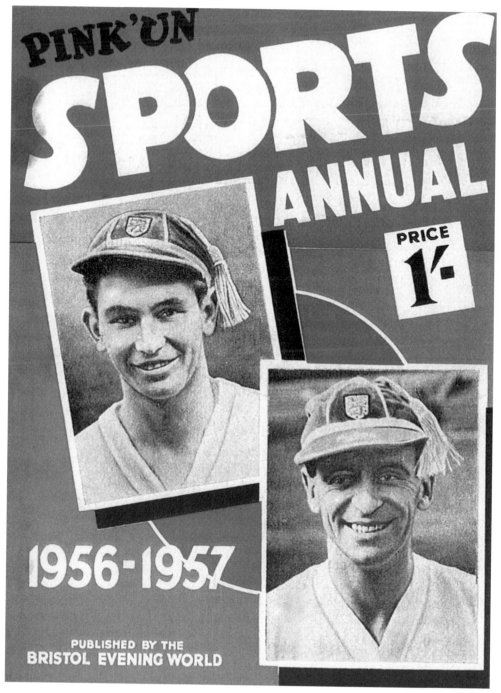

John Atyeo and Bradford, who had both won England caps, were featured on the front of the *Bristol Evening World Pink 'Un Sports Annual* for 1956/57.

Rovers reached the quarter-final of the competition. Unlike 1950/51, they only had to progress from the third round, by virtue of their Second Division status, but like the previous quarter-final appearance the run was to end in a 3–1 defeat. The FA Cup journey began with a convincing 5–0 victory over Third Division (North) side Mansfield Town, four Rovers forwards (but not Bradford) getting on the scoresheet, with the reward for this a home tie with high-riding First Division Burnley and a crowd of 34,229 attracted to Eastville. Burnley boasted famous names such as England 'B' international and centre-half Jimmy Adamson and Jimmy McIlroy, an inside forward who won 55 caps for Northern Ireland. Yet, for the second time in three years, Rovers were to defeat top division opponents. A 2–2 draw meant a potentially tough replay at Turf Moor, but Rovers emerged 3–2 victors, Norman Sykes scoring his first goal for a year and Dai Ward adding a couple. This was a staggering achievement for Rovers to have accomplished and it remained the only occasion that the club had won any fixture before a crowd of over 40,000, until the League Two play-off final against Shrewsbury Town at Wembley in 2007. Supporters of football in Bristol could not believe their luck as Rovers and City were drawn together in the fifth round of the competition. An attendance of 39,126 at Ashton Gate brought gate receipts of £5,439 and witnessed arguably the most exciting of all Bristol derby matches, with seven goals, a missed penalty and a highly controversial Geoff Bradford winner 7 minutes from time. Rovers should have taken a first-minute lead, but it was John Watkins who scored against his former club 3 minutes later to give City an early lead.

Geoff Bradford (on ground) and Barrie Meyer just fail to connect with a cross to the relief of Bristol City goalkeeper Bob Anderson in the thrilling fifth round FA Cup tie.

By half time Sykes, Ward and Barrie Meyer had scored, Ron Nicholls had saved a penalty from Watkins and Rovers led 3–1. However, City recovered to level at 3–3 and, with a quarter-final place up for grabs Ward's through-ball to Bradford 7 minutes from time brought Rovers a 4–3 victory. City were convinced that Bradford's winning goal was offside, but this is how he saw it: 'We were under pressure when Dai Ward broke away with me on the right. Mike Thresher, City's left-back, was covering me, but as Dai went on he had to leave me and go to Dai. I kept behind Dai all the time, and the linesman was right with me. Dai slipped the ball to me and I hit it past Bob Anderson as he came out to meet me. I know I wasn't offside.'

The second quarter-final in Rovers' FA Cup history was an all-Second Division affair. However, despite a Bradford goal to parallel the one he had scored in February 1951, Fulham ran out clear winners. Jimmy Hill put Fulham ahead from a rebound after his 9th minute shot had been blocked, and Arthur Stevens, whose goals had knocked Rovers out of the FA Cup in 1948, added close-range goals after 12 and 35 minutes. At the kick-off, a Rovers supporter had run onto the pitch, dribbled the ball and scored, but all Rovers had to cheer was a classic Bradford header from Sykes' 68th-minute free kick, although in Rovers' next attack he did scrape the bar.

Rovers' first team, 1959/60. Back row, left to right: Ray Mabbutt, Norman Sykes, Malcolm Norman, David Pyle, Doug Hillard, Josser Watling. Front row: Granville Smith, Alfie Biggs, Geoff Bradford, Dai Ward, Peter Hooper.

The extended cup run distracted the Rovers side somewhat from its attempt to reach the First Division and in another high-scoring season, Rovers scored 85 goals and conceded 80, finishing tenth in Division Two, as Bradford top-scored with 20 goals in 33 league matches. Two Bradford goals helped defeat Blackburn Rovers 4–0 at the start of the season, while another Bradford double eased Rovers towards a 3–3 draw with Bristol City in April, where all six goals were scored in an extraordinary first half. The sides met again in the Gloucestershire FA Senior Cup final, where City won 4–1, as well as hitting the woodwork twice, after Bradford had put Rovers in front from a Biggs pass after only 6 minutes. If FA Cup attendances were high, then so too were those in the league, where the golden years of post-war football coupled with Rovers' years of relative success combined to boost crowd figures.

Support throughout the 1957/58 season was good, the average home gate amounting to 22,166, and for a sixth consecutive season, the average attendance at Eastville topped 20,000, yet this was also the final such season in the twentieth century. It is a matter of special interest that the average attendance for reserve matches that season was the highest ever attained in the club's history – 5,288 (an increase of 600 per match on the previous season's figures).

On 31 October 1958 the Bristol public were shocked to hear of the untimely death of Rovers stalwart Harry Bamford, who tragically died from injuries sustained when his motorcycle was in collision with a car in Clifton three days earlier as he returned from coaching boys at Clifton College.

The veteran full-back, aged 38, had been at Eastville since December 1945, having joined Rovers when demobilised from the army, making his first-team debut the following August. For nine seasons from 1949/50 he had been a team-mate of Bradford during Bristol Rovers' halcyon days of the 1950s. In fact, the two Bristolians appeared in 301 league and cup games together wearing the famous blue-and-white quartered shirts, Bamford having made 486 appearances for Rovers prior to that fateful October day. As a tribute to him,

Bristol-born full-back Harry Bamford died tragically on 31 October 1958 at the age of 38 following an accident while riding his motorcycle in Clifton. Bamford made 486 appearances for Rovers, the second most in the club's history. Bradford and Bamford made over 300 appearances in the same Rovers side.

the Harry Bamford Memorial Trophy was donated anonymously as an annual award 'to a player who has upheld the tradition of sportsmanship created by Harry Bamford'. Geoff was honoured by being the first recipient of the trophy which was presented to him by Bamford's widow, Violet, at a match in aid of the Bamford Fund, set up by Rovers for his dependants, which was played between Arsenal and a Combined Bristol XI on the evening of Friday 8 May 1959. The crowd of 28,347 set a record for a non-competitive game at Eastville with gate receipts of more than £3,500. The team fielded by Arsenal included internationals Mel Charles, Dave Bowen and Tommy Docherty. Charles, who had recently become the costliest player in British football in moving from Swansea for £42,750, plus two Arsenal reserves, had yet to make his Arsenal debut when the Gunners visited Eastville. Also in the Arsenal line-up was Vic Groves, the former Leyton Orient winger, who had been a member of the FA party, with Bradford, which toured the West Indies in 1955. The combined side comprising six Rovers players (Geoff Bradford, Peter Hooper, Ray Mabbutt, Norman Sykes, Dai Ward and Josser Watling) and five from City (John Atyeo, Tommy Burden, Tony Cook, Wally Hinshelwood and Alan Williams) triumphed by 5 goals to 4. Bradford scored two of the Combined Bristol side's goals, with two more from his good friend John Atyeo, plus one from Dai Ward. Bradford gave his side the lead after 8 minutes when he accepted a long pass from Sykes and left Sims, in the Arsenal goal, standing with a left-foot diagonal shot to the right corner of the net. After 20 minutes, Bradford scored again to make it 3–0. From Cook the ball went to Williams. Docherty misjudged it badly, and Bradford, racing through the opposition placed the ball to Sims' right as the goalkeeper came out. According to a local newspaper match report, 'exhibition football – some of it of the highest class – enraptured the crowd at Eastville last night and made this match for the Harry Bamford Fund a memorable occasion.' As the final whistle went, Rovers secretary John Gummow asked over the public address system for silence and announced that Geoff Bradford was the first winner of the Harry Bamford Memorial Trophy, much to the delight of the 28,000 spectators who must have felt that no Bristol professional more richly deserved the accolade.

Surrounded by well-wishers in the Rovers dressing-room, Bradford asked John Coe to thank the committee who made the award for bestowing him an honour he would prize above all others. 'Harry was a close friend, and I'm really thrilled to be the first person to hold the trophy presented in his memory,' said the delighted recipient. The committee of six consisted of Mr Newman, Chairman of the Gloucestershire FA, Herbert Hampden Alpass (Chairman of Bristol Rovers), Harry Dolman (Chairman of Bristol City) and three sports editors of local newspapers.

The chairman of the committee was Mr W.E. Pinnell, former sports editor of the *Bristol Evening Post*, who represented the donor of the trophy, which stands 11ins high and was provided by Kemp Bros. of Union Street, Bristol. Bradford also received a certificate, designed by and executed by Denis Curthoys of the *Bristol Evening Post*.

1958/59 was a mixed season for Rovers, for they neither won nor lost three consecutive league fixtures all season, which kept them just on the fringe of the promotion places throughout the campaign, but in finishing sixth in Division Two there were indeed

"AIN'T LIFE FUN!"

RIDING high are Bristol Rovers in their second year in Second Division football and the Tann lads are playing good football and testing the best of them.

Team work and club spirit are some of the key factors in the current bright look of the Rovers plus, of course, a brilliant young player by the name of Geoff Brad-ford. When Geoff isn't scoring goals he is making them for others and enjoying every minute of it.

Our photographer peeped into the dressing room recently and met some of the Bristol Rovers lads. He also caught the excellent study (above) of Geoff Bradford (left) sharing a joke with genial Harry Bamford, that sterling defender who is such a popular performer at Eastville.

Geoff and his good friend and team-mate Harry Bamford were featured sharing a joke in the October 1954 edition of *Soccer Star* magazine.

Goalmouth action against Scunthorpe United in the opening match of the 1958/59 season, with Bradford hitting a right-foot shot at the visitors' goal. One of the familiar Eastville Stadium flower beds is visible behind the goal.

grounds for optimism. Rovers won their final three home games, each time defeating sides (Liverpool, Charlton Athletic and Sheffield Wednesday) with larger reputations and greater spending power and which had beaten Rovers earlier in the season.

The team performance of the season was against Grimsby Town at Eastville in the middle of November. A masterful 7–3 victory, the only occasion Rovers have won by this scoreline in league football, made light of the fact that they had lost their two previous home games. After a quiet start, the match exploded into life just before half time, as Dai Ward, after 28 minutes, and Peter Hooper, 11 minutes later, gave Rovers a 2–0 lead, only for Tommy Briggs, whose seven goals for Blackburn Rovers had sunk the Eastville side in February 1955, to pull one back a minute before half time. Ward extended Rovers' lead and Mike Cullen replied for Grimsby before two Hooper goals in 4 minutes completed his hat-trick and left Rovers 5–2 ahead. Undeterred, Ron Rafferty scored 14 minutes from time. Geoff Bradford, however, scored twice in 5 minutes and Rovers had avenged the 7–0 drubbing of eleven months earlier. Rovers' sixth goal after 84 minutes gave Bradford his 199th league and cup goal for the Pirates. Ward drew the goalkeeper out of his goal before crossing from the goal line a perfect centre to Bradford, who only had to tap the ball into an empty net, and 5 minutes later came his 200th senior goal.

Bradford's greatest personal performance, however, came against Rotherham United at Eastville in March. Rovers' 'Hat-trick Hero' had scored ten league hat-tricks for Rovers, but never before four times in one match. Bradford had missed the 3–3 draw at Millmoor in October and, returning after injury only a week before this return fixture, had in fact not scored in the first team since Boxing Day in a 2–0 victory at Ipswich. As a warm-up to his remarkable achievement, Bradford scored four goals for Rovers reserves against Swansea Town reserves in a 4–2 away victory on 21 February. A first-minute goal a month later set him on his way and he contributed all his side's goals as Rovers recorded a 4–1 victory on 14 March over a Rotherham side one place off the bottom of the table. The first Rovers player to score four times in a match in the Second Division, he was also the first to achieve this feat since Vic Lambden on Easter Monday 1952. Finding the clinging mud just the conditions to suit him, Bradford rolled back the years at Eastville and treated one of the smallest crowds of the season to the kind of display that gained for him his England cap. Within a minute of the start Bradford scored with a simple low shot from McIlvenny's pass, then 2 minutes after the restart Bradford signalled to Len Drake, telling him where he wanted the ball. Drake obliged, Bradford ran onto the pass and shot under goalkeeper John Quairney's diving body into the net. Completing his hat-trick after 52 minutes, his angled shot from Biggs's pass left Quairney standing and in the 67th minute from Hooper's opening Bradford side-footed the ball home with the ease of a craftsman.

At the end of the game he walked off to an ovation from supporters sitting in the centre of the South Stand that must have sounded like sweet music in his ears. This was the old polished Bradford – passes of slide-rule accuracy, astute positional sense, clever switching of attack, economy of movement, lethal shooting. Rovers assistant manger Fred Ford who was looking after things in the absence of his chief Bert Tann had this to say, 'We always knew that Geoff Bradford had a lot of football still in him. We could see it in practice games. It was good to see him getting goals again. Now it is up to him to show that he

Bradford followed by team-mates Barrie Meyer and Peter Hooper run on to the pitch at Fulham, 1 March 1958.

can still make a contribution to Bristol Rovers. I am certain he can.' Sheffield Wednesday, the new champions, were defeated in the final match of the season by a Bradford goal, struck venomously from Doug Hillard's through-ball after 11 minutes, the 200th league goal of his Rovers career and his twentieth of the season to leave him as the club's second highest scorer, behind 26-goal Dai Ward. Hillard made the opening with a lobbed pass which found Bradford, and although Peter Swan, the visitors' centre-half, pushed him in the back, the Rovers leader was able to put in a fierce drive. Goalkeeper Roy MacLaren tried to palm the ball away but it was travelling too quickly for him, and spun off his hands into the net, in what was an excellent example of how deadly Bradford could still be in the penalty area. There was some concern for Bradford a minute or so later, when he hurt his face in a collision with MacLaren after meeting a centre from Smith. It proved to be nothing much, but subsequently he hurt his ribs, and in the dressing room after the game was over he had to be strapped up by the Eastville club's trainer. Rovers should have increased their lead after 30 minutes, when a power shot by Bradford looked a certain winner, but MacLaren rose to full height and tipped the ball over – a fine shot was matched by an equally fine save. With a 2–1 victory Rovers equalled their previous highest final placing in Division Two, obtained in 1955/56, and enabled Rovers to equal their previous best Second Division aggregate points (48), achieved in the same season.

At the beginning of the 1959/60 season Rovers were among the first clubs in the country to name their team for the opening match of the season, and at 31, Bradford had come through the long weeks of the gruelling seaside training camp at Weston-super-Mare so well that he was given the no. 9 shirt without hesitation. 1959/60 opened with a six-match unbeaten run, but as the season progressed Rovers suffered several heavy defeats. Four or more goals were conceded on six occasions as the Pirates finished the season in ninth place in Division Two. Twelve goals in 34 league appearances saw Bradford as joint third top scorer with Dai Ward, behind Alfie Biggs (22) and Peter Hooper (13). In the fourth round of the FA Cup Rovers were paired with Preston North End, where Tom Finney was outstanding in a 5–1 replay win at Deepdale, following a 3–3 draw at Eastville in which Bradford was concussed in the first half and remembered little of the second.

With the scores level he had a good chance to score the winner, but shot from long range when he had plenty of time to go nearer the goal and shoot. In addition to his twelve league goals, Bradford played at centre forward in five Football Combination appearances and managed to score two goals on three occasions.

In high-scoring reserve games he netted a brace against Plymouth in a 4–3 defeat at Home Park in November, a further two against Notts County in a remarkable 9–4 victory at Eastville on 5 December, and scored both goals in the away fixture as County took revenge by winning 5–4 in April. At the end of the season Rovers played Bristol Rugby Club on 4 May in an experimental game of 'Socby'. After a goalless first half, Bradford scored twice and Hooper once to give Rovers a 3–1 win, with the rugby club's captain John Blake scoring a consolation goal.

With the benefit of hindsight, the end of the 1950s can be seen to have drawn to a close the golden years in the Bristol Rovers story, although Bert Tann was beginning again to weave together a team of young, predominantly Bristolian footballers. But it is all too often the case with a relatively small club that the threat of relegation is never too far away. While Rovers had finished in the top ten in Division Two for seven consecutive seasons, there was now no money for purchasing replacements for older players. With the familiar names of George Petherbridge, Alfie Biggs, Geoff Bradford, Dai Ward and Peter Hooper, the sole

Geoff Bradford presents the Harry Bamford Memorial Trophy to Colin Mitchell of Clifton St Vincents after the match between Bristol Rovers and Swedish club Djurgårdens on 28 March 1960.

ever-present, in the forward line, it was a very recognisable Rovers attack which began the 1960/61 season, but as a younger generation of Bristolians came through the ranks the club slipped to a final league placing of seventeenth and two long, trying years lay ahead.

Twenty league defeats was the club's worst record since 1947/48 and 92 goals conceded the most since 1935/36. Rovers finished the season just four positions and four points above relegated Portsmouth as the 1960/61 season reached its finale. A final nine league appearances brought to a conclusion the long and reliable career of wing-half Peter Sampson, leaving just Bradford and Petherbridge of the championship-winning side. Bradford made 32 league appearances scoring 12 goals from the centre forward position, the only double coming in the 4–1 home defeat of Luton Town on 25 February. However, even in the later stage of his career his reputation as a 'hat-trick hero' was maintained as was demonstrated on 12 November 1960 at Home Park when he scored four goals from the inside right position playing for Rovers reserves against Plymouth Argyle in a 5–2 victory. In front of 1,955 spectators Bradford taught the younger Plymouth side a lesson in the art of scheming and goalscoring on the pitch where he had suffered his first serious injury a few seasons earlier. In the 5th minute he opened the scoring when he ran through a helpless defence to shoot into an empty net. But Bradford really came in to his own with a superb second-half hat-trick, composed of goals in the 54th, 70th and 87th minutes. Giving Bradford extra support was right-winger Harold Jarman, and together this pair proved the most dangerous combination on the field.

Rovers made history in September 1960 by hosting and winning the first game ever played in the newly created Football League Cup. By dint of a 7.15 p.m. kick-off, 15 minutes

earlier than other ties, Fulham's Maurice Cook is credited with the tournament's first goal and Rovers, with Jarman scoring for the club for the first time, with the opening victory. In the first half, with Fulham leading 1–0, Bradford shot with tremendous power from Hooper's through pass. Once again goalkeeper Ken Hewkins was beaten and once again Jim Langley kicked the ball off the line. In the 59th minute, Bradford produced the evening's highlight by scoring the winning goal. Peter Hooper harassed full-back George Cohen into making a short pass back and in a flash Bradford was on to the ball and took it around Hewkins. He then rammed the ball into the net from an acute angle off centre-half Roy Bentley's

A fine action shot of Geoff Bradford, c. 1960.

arm as George Cohen made a despairing tackle. Six years later the hapless defender ended up winning a World Cup winner's medal.

Of all the players who were with Bristol Rovers during Bert Tann's time at the club, Geoff Bradford was surely just about the last one who could be expected to have to face the threat of being ostracised by his team-mates. Yet that is precisely what happened when the Association Football Players' & Trainers' Union, popularly known as the Players' Union, proposed strike action in their attempt to do away with the maximum wage at the beginning of the 1960s. Despite the previous valiant efforts of the Footballers Players' Union there had been no changes to their main employment terms and conditions until 1945 when the maximum close season wage was increased to £7 per week. Two years later a National Arbitration Tribunal was established. It decided that the maximum wage should be raised to £12 in the playing season and £10 in the close season. The minimum wage for players over 20 was set at £7. By the time Bradford had entered the world of professional football in 1949 the maximum wage was increased to £14, rising to £15 (1953), £17 (1957) and £20 (1958). The union argued that in 1939 the footballers' £8 was approximately double the average industrial wage; by 1960 the gap had narrowed to £5 with these figures standing at £20 and £15 respectively. The clubs had a lot of influence on the players and a retained system was in common use. If a player was unhappy with his wages or not playing on a regular basis he could ask for a transfer and the club would set a fee which needed to be matched by the buying club. The maximum wage meant there really was not much advantage for a player to move to another part of the country. It was not uncommon for many to spend their entire careers at the same club. There was 100 per cent membership of the union at Eastville, where all the players were prepared to support a strike – except for Bradford (Membership No. 554) and Ray Mabbutt, who both felt that the maximum wage should be raised but could see the dangers of abolishing it altogether. When, however, it came to everyone stating firmly whether to strike or not, Mabbutt decided that he would support the union's action if it became necessary.

Bradford was therefore left out on a limb, and that was when he was told that if it came to a strike, and he still kept the same attitude, the other players would refuse to play with him in the same team. 'There weren't many of the old brigade left at Eastville by then,' he said in recalling the unpleasant incident many years later. 'Two new generations of players had come into the team, and they had a different approach to football than I did. Our attitudes became so far apart that I was called a "blackleg". I was 33, and all I wanted to do was carry on playing football. But I was also concerned about what the changes could do to the game, not just to older players like myself but to the youngsters as well. Obviously, I didn't like being called a blackleg, but it didn't worry me, and in the end my firm stand gave some of the younger players' second thoughts. They began to see what I was driving at.' Alfie Biggs was the union's representative at Eastville and on his return from meetings would keep his colleagues up to date with what was happening at PFA meetings and the discussions that were taking place. What he had to say made Bradford feel that decisions were being made without sufficient thought being given to the consequences. His recollections of his fears at the time make prophetic reading regarding the modern game,

Bradford in the early 1960s.

'My concern was not so much what a player could earn in the course of a season or two, but what his life span in the game was going to be,' he explained. 'The post-war boom was over, and if clubs were going to have to pay players a lot more money then there would be room for fewer players in the game. It was as simple as that to me, and I have been proved right. I saw it affecting players at both ends of the scale. The older player kept on to help bring on young players in the reserves – he would go,' which was exactly the fate that befell Bradford at the end of his illustrious career. 'And so would the younger players who had ability but needed to be given time for it to be brought out. Clubs would not be able to afford to give them time. I was also concerned about what too much money would do to the game itself. I could see it bringing an end to artistry in football. The game has become a means of earning big money, in which players can not afford to lose games, so they can't afford to express their talents. I could see it wrecking the kind of team spirit we had known at Eastville. Football is a team game, so everyone in the team should be the same.' Following talks involving the PFA, the Football Association, the Football League and the Ministry of Labour, the Football League committee offered a gradual increase in the maximum wage to £30, taking place over five years, but at a PFA meeting in London, 250 players voted unanimously for strike action. Two further meetings elsewhere in the country brought the total to 712 players, of whom 18 voted against strike action. On 9 January 1961 the Football League made a revised proposal, which PFA members rejected by a three to one margin. But on 18 January the parties agreed to an immediate abolition of the maximum wage and the planned strike was called off three days before it was due to take place. How right Bradford was in seeing that Rovers would be among the clubs particularly hard-hit by the release of the purse strings. The 'No Buy, No Sell' policy Rovers adopted after the Second World War to stop the drain of outstanding talent away from Eastville was doomed from the moment when players were no longer all bound by the maximum wage. Loyalties were tested to the limit, and it was no mere coincidence that the first full season after the introduction of the new deal for players ended with Rovers' loss of their hard-won Second Division status. During the summer close season, when footballers received reduced wages, to help bring in additional money for his young family Geoff drove a van delivering lemonade to shops and houses throughout the Bristol area, at times allowing his three daughters, Lesley, Lynn and Nichola, to accompany him on his rounds.

7

RELEGATION AND THE GREAT ESCAPE

The first signs of a troubled season were apparent in the early weeks of the 1961/62 campaign. Liverpool under up-and-coming manager Bill Shankly, who apparently had made an abortive attempt to sign Geoff Bradford for the Merseysiders, came to Eastville on the opening day of the season and won 2–0 with their new signings Ian St John, Ron Yeats and Gordon Milne making successful debuts. Liverpool gained promotion at the end of the campaign while Rovers were relegated. After losing their first seven matches of the season to Liverpool, Bury (twice), Rotherham, Sunderland, Scunthorpe and Stoke City, it created an unwelcome Rovers record, something which the club found difficult to recover from. That was followed by three consecutive wins, all at home against Leyton Orient, Scunthorpe, and an impressive 4–0 thumping of Leeds United. Bradford contributed three goals in those opening ten fixtures as Rovers scored a dozen goals and conceded 18. Bradford began the season at centre forward playing in 21 consecutive games scoring 8 times, but by Christmas was switched to right full-back (playing 14 matches in that position) – with the ever-reliable Ray Mabbutt leading the line – except for a handful of sporadic appearances leading the attack again.

It was difficult for any Rovers supporter to admit this, but Geoff Bradford was no longer the prolific, potent goalscorer he had once been. The five hat-tricks in 1953/54, the two goals in each of four consecutive games in October 1954 and the England cap were a thing of the past. He had scored 12 league goals in 1959/60, two against Stoke City in February being his only brace of the season and 12 more league goals came the following season. The only survivor from the early days of the Tann regime and still a regular in the side during 1960/61, Bradford had struck up a useful partnership with Alfie Biggs, but with Biggs transferred to Preston North End in July 1961 he found it much harder going.

As the team continued to struggle, never higher than seventeenth place, from the Boxing Day home defeat by Brighton, Rovers suffered nine defeats and just five wins in their final nineteen league games of the 1961/62 season. On Good Friday, Rovers drew with a Charlton Athletic side forced to play inside forward John Hewie in goal. Twenty-four hours later and back at centre forward, Bradford's two goals earned a draw with Walsall which left Rovers and Leeds United with two matches remaining on 33 points, above Swansea Town now with a game in hand on 32, and a rejuvenated Brighton on 31. On Easter Monday, as Rovers and Brighton lost, Swansea picked up a point. Against Charlton Athletic on 23 April

Rovers' squad, 1961/62. Back row, left to right: Doug Hillard, John Frowen, Norman Sykes, Malcolm Norman, Jackie Pitt (coach), Howard Radford, David Pyle, Terry Oldfield, David Head. Middle row: Josser Watling, Ray Mabbutt, Harold Jarman, Bobby Jones, Geoff Bradford, Peter Hooper, John Watkins, Brian Carter. Front row: Joe Davis, Mike Slocombe, George Petherbridge, Dave Stone, Roy James, Arthur Hall.

Rovers defeated Leeds United 4–0 at Eastville on 23 September 1961. Here Peter Hooper (far right) scores, with Bradford in close attendance. Hooper netted two with Bradford and Bobby Jones adding two others.

the score was 1–1 in the dying minutes when a fluke goal by Stuart Leary gave the Valiants both points. This was how Bradford recalled Rovers' footballing catastrophe: 'Stuart had the ball on the right and intended to pull back a centre from the by-line. But he mis-hit the ball, and Howard Radford, taken by surprise, was beaten as the ball squeezed between him and the near post. Stuart was very apologetic; upset that a goal like that had probably put us down.' Twenty-four hours later Leeds United drew with Bury and the Swans beat Plymouth Argyle 5–0. Brighton were relegated and Swansea safe while, with one game left, the remaining relegation place was to be taken by Leeds, on 34 points, or Rovers, a point below them.

As Leeds faced the daunting task of visiting Newcastle United, Rovers had to beat Luton Town, a side they had earlier defeated at Eastville. At Kenilworth Road, however, Gordon Turner put the Hatters ahead after 3 minutes, following a poor goal-kick by Howard Radford, and Alec Ashworth's shot 12 minutes later was deflected in off Dave Bumpstead so that Rovers, in losing 2–0, were relegated with Brighton to Division Three, three points adrift of Leeds United who had managed to win 3–0 at St James's Park. Incredibly, above Leeds and Swansea were eight clubs on 39 points. Crucially, Rovers had won only twice in the sixteen fixtures against these sides, and there were no wins in their final five matches, which was just not good enough. Rovers scored 53 league goals, the lowest figure in the Second Division years, where the club had previously reached 80 in four consecutive seasons. Twenty-four players were used during the season with six debutants; Bert Tann had introduced several new signings including John Hills and Brian Carter, but the side struggled. The only ever-present was left full-back John Frowen who completed a run of 66 consecutive league appearances. Bradford missed just three games. Meanwhile veteran winger George Petherbridge, who had played in 452 league matches and scored in the first sixteen consecutive post-war seasons, played his final game for the club on 30 December at Brighton. Bobby Jones, with one more goal than Bradford and Peter Hooper, was top scorer on 13 league goals. For the third season in succession Bradford scored a dozen league goals, a remarkable return considering Rovers' relegation and of his 39 league appearances 14 were at right full-back. Braces were scored against Sunderland at Eastville in September, in a 2–0 November victory at Southampton, and on 21 April, both goals in the 2–2 Eastville draw with Walsall. He also managed League Cup goals in both rounds of the competition that Rovers were involved in, the winner against Hartlepool United in the first round victory and Rovers' goal in the 1–1 home draw with Blackburn Rovers on 2 October in the next round. The slump back to the Third Division prompted a number of changes at the club that summer, the distinctive strip being one of the scapegoats as for the start of the next season Rovers ditched their familiar quartered shirts which they adopted in 1931 in favour of a short-lived white top with blue pinstripes. With the loss of Second Division status the door closed on what was arguably one of the most entertaining and memorable periods in Bristol Rovers' long history.

The signs of a struggling side were evident to be seen by all as the older players from the successful late 1950s side either left or retired. Manager Bert Tann's search for replacements after many years as a club with a 'No Buy, No Sell' policy proved to be mixed. Local recruits from the youth and reserve teams were coming through but with little money spent

Rovers players Slocombe, Jarman, Williams and Mabbutt celebrate a Peter Hooper goal against Preston North End on 24 February 1962 in a 2–1 win. Bradford (far left) was nearing the end of his career and playing at right full-back.

on transfer fees the side struggled for the second consecutive season and, indeed came within minutes of a disastrous second successive relegation into the uncharted waters of Division Four. Tann had appointed Bill Dodgin as chief scout in 1961 and in July 1962 he promoted Bobby Campbell to the post of coach. A fast raiding winger with Chelsea and Reading, Campbell had won two Scottish caps and was manager at Dumbarton before joining Rovers. Both Dodgin and Campbell were to manage Rovers in their own right but, for now, their brief was to rebuild the club from the ashes of relegation. There was clearly insufficient talent on Rovers' books and no money to purchase replacements, so their task was to work with the many local footballers, searching for the rare glimpse of raw skill or character which would enable a young player to break into league football. Many evenings were spent carefully building up the skills of numerous players under the dim floodlights of the Muller Road car park ash practice pitch. The departure of winger George Petherbridge to Salisbury City left Geoff Bradford as the sole survivor of the Division Three (South) days. Doug Hillard, Norman Sykes, Ray Mabbutt, Harold Jarman and Bobby Jones were all by now experienced Rovers players. The new goalkeeper, with Howard Radford retired, was Esmond Million, signed for £5,000 from Middlesbrough and Rovers were able to benefit from the experience of the previous season's signing, Keith Williams, from Plymouth Argyle.

Rovers changed their shirts from blue-and-white quarters to a thin blue-and-white pinstripe for the start of the 1962/63 season. Back row, left to right: Ryden, Gardiner, Stone, Hendy, Hillard, Baker. Middle row: Bradford, Bumpstead, Sykes, Million, Hall, Humes, Frowen, Jones G. Front row: Slocombe, Oldfield, Jones K., Mabbutt, Hamilton, Williams, Jarman, Jones R., Davis.

Also the popular Bristol-born centre forward Alfie Biggs returned in October in a £12,000 deal, 'The Baron' coming back to Eastville after fifteen months away. Not long after Biggs returned to Rovers from Preston North End, and after one bad result, manager Bert Tann told the players that as a punishment they would have to do a cross-country run. They all trooped off leaving Eastville Park across the Purdown countryside and as the players spread out even the younger players found it was a testing run, but lo and behold one of the first ones back was Alfie Biggs. Not normally noted for his great running ability Biggs turned up at Eastville where Tann and his coaches were waiting for them all to return. One of the Rovers directors then arrived by car at the stadium to inform Tann that he had seen Biggs in his full training kit and boots getting off a bus at the bottom of Muller Road! Biggs was reprimanded by Tann and told to do extra runs.

Bradford started the 1962/63 season at centre forward for the first three games, but was then switched to play at right full-back in favour of Doug Hillard for fourteen consecutive games, scoring the first goal of just two he managed that season – a penalty at Southend in a 3–2 defeat. He lost his place following that defeat and failed to make another first team appearance until 29 April when he was used as an emergency centre-half in the 5–0 defeat at Coventry City. Geoff finished the season on the left wing in three of the final four crucial

Bradford challenges Millwall goalkeeper Bill Glazier during Rovers' 2–0 win over Crystal Palace at Eastville on 25 August 1962.

games of the weather-delayed season, scoring his second goal of that struggling campaign in a vital 2–0 home win over Colchester United on 14 May and featured in the crucial win at Halifax in the penultimate game of the season. From the time of his step down from the first team in October until his late reinstatement to the senior side for the crucial relegation battles, Bradford made ten appearances for the reserves in the Football Combination and had five outings for Rovers in the Western League during 1962/63. Bradford had been spotted by Rovers while playing for Soundwell in the Western League some thirteen years earlier and by a twist of fate Rovers played their Western League home fixtures at Frenchay, the village that had been home to Bradford during his formative years. The Western League game against Bath City reserves on 17 November, at Frenchay, was one of the very few games that he featured as right-half in a Rovers side, and on his 'home turf' Bradford scored his final hat-trick for Rovers when, on 8 December 1962, he netted all three goals in a 5–3 defeat of Bideford.

On the morning of Saturday 27 April 1963, and with the battle against relegation not yet won, Rovers suspended two of its first-team players, an action which caused a sensation in English football. The two Rovers players involved were goalkeeper Esmond Million and inside forward Keith Williams, who the *People* newspaper accused of accepting bribes to 'throw' the relegation clash with Bradford Park Avenue on 20 April. The club wasted no time in suspending both players in whom Rovers had invested £11,500 in transfer fees, with Williams at the time of his suspension Rovers' leading goalscorer with 17 goals. It transpired that goalkeeper Million had accepted a £300 bribe to enable Bradford Park Avenue to beat Rovers, and had allowed a back-pass to slip past him and let a cross go, leaving the innocent Kevin Hector to score twice. The match had been drawn 2–2, so Million and his accomplice Williams, who also admitted trying to fix the outcome, had received none of the money. The Mansfield Town defender Brian Phillips, a former team-mate of Million at Middlesbrough, was named as the 'fixer', working on behalf of a syndicate of professional gamblers.

The disgraced Rovers pair and Phillips were fined a nominal £50 each at Doncaster Magistrates Court in July 1963 and banned from football for life by the Football Association. Phillips was later sentenced at Nottingham Assizes to fifteen months' imprisonment. Williams was to resurface in South African football which, at that time lay outside the remit of FIFA, the world football governing body. The press also uncovered details of how they had unsuccessfully tried to persuade Rovers' full-back Gwyn Jones to join them in the match-fixing attempt. Suddenly Rovers were making national headlines for all the wrong reasons. The image of professional football had been tarnished, but Rovers' immediate response to the crisis and the way the club had responded and helped bring the culprits to justice came in for high praise. Rovers were left to survive the relegation dogfight without two key players, but with a clear conscience that the club was working hard to stamp out all that was unsavoury in the game.

Bradford takes on the Wrexham defence at Eastville on 11 May 1963 during the extended season caused by the icy weather which saw Rovers unable to play any matches from 16 December until 9 February.

Rovers' draw at Bradford left both clubs on the brink of the drop into Division Four. The winter of 1962/63 was one of the worst in the twentieth century as far as the weather was concerned, with snow lying for weeks, and as a result of the atrocious weather, Rovers extraordinarily played nine league games in April and five in May. Bradford and Biggs had scored to beat Colchester United on 14 May, leaving Rovers requiring victory over Halifax Town at The Shay to avoid relegation, prior to the final game which was lost 2–0 at Port Vale. A narrow 3–2 win at Halifax avoided the prospect of double relegation, yet it was a close call. A miserly crowd of 2,126, albeit boosted by some 500 enthusiastic Rovers supporters, saw Rovers a goal ahead after 2 minutes through Bobby Jones' shot and 2–0 up 10 minutes later when Ian Hamilton headed home Bradford's cross. The two-goal advantage could have been increased to five by half time, when Jones had chances to complete a hat-trick, and Bradford missed what he admitted afterwards was an easy opportunity. However, already-relegated Halifax recovered after half time and quickly equalised through shots from Paddy Stanley and Dennis Fidler. With just 14 minutes remaining, Rovers won a corner and Jones' kick found Hamilton who half-headed, half-shouldered the winner to ensure Third Division survival. In the end Rovers finished the season in nineteenth place with 41 points, one ahead of Reading, who survived only because of a goal average that was superior to Bradford Park Avenue's, with Halifax, Carlisle, Brighton, and Bradford all relegated. The Yorkshire club whose match with Rovers had caused such a footballing furore also finished the campaign with 41 points, and one can only contemplate what the final league positions might have been if Million and Williams had not succumbed to temptation.

8

THE TWILIGHT YEARS

Despite his advancing years Bradford was still a tremendous asset to Bristol Rovers. In fact during 1962/63 he occupied nine different positions for one Rovers team or another.

In 1963/64, Bradford, at 36 years of age, was in what would have been his third benefit season. His return to the first team for its fourth match – at Shrewsbury – marked his 500th overall appearance and he had the added satisfaction of scoring the last of his 242 league goals when he found the net in each half of a 4–0 home win against Bristol City that December in the 50th league meeting between the clubs. It was fitting that the veteran Bradford, written off by many in Bristol two years earlier, should contribute two goals in the Golden Jubilee battle of Bristol. The first after just 4 minutes was an opportunist goal as goalkeeper Mike Gibson and defender Gordon Low blundered following Ray Mabbutt's fiercely struck free kick. At the time the goal was credited as an own goal to both Low and Gibson, but Bradford had no doubt that he scored, 'I don't mess about with those sort of chances,' he said. 'Sure the ball was going in, but it had not crossed the line until I finally kicked it into the net.' Just before the end Ian Hamilton gained space down the right and placed a superb ball right on Bradford's head for him to score with a glorious header. There were probably not many in the 19,451 crowd gathered at Eastville on 14 December 1963, nor among the thousands of readers who subsequently pored over the match reports, who realised the quirk of fate that Bradford's goalscoring swansong was achieved against the club who missed the opportunity to sign him back in 1949. Just one more strike into the City net would have been the perfect finale for the 'Hat-Trick Hero', but it was not to be. There were still a number of appearances before the end of the season, six in the league but no further goals. Alfie Biggs, appointed captain on his return from Preston, was an ever-present in 1963/64 and his overall total of 37 goals broke the Rovers record for one season that Bradford had held for eleven years. Bradford, whose last season it was to be, retained the league best with his 1952/53 tally of 33 to the 30 of Biggs.

At Coventry City on 23 November 1963 Bradford was a defender in the 4–2 defeat by the eventual champions, but 'two goals by the best centre-forward in the Third Division (Geoff Hudson) was no reflection on Bradford's play at centre-half. His heading strength was needed too in view of Terry Oldfield's absence, and he was calm and resolute in his tackling and clearances.' During the week there was much discussion in the *Bristol Evening*

Geoff Bradford enjoyed fifteen seasons with Rovers, his last team photograph was in 1963/64. Back row, left to right: Geoff Bradford, Doug Hillard, Bernard Hall, Gwyn Jones, Ray Mabbutt. Middle row: Bert Tann (manager), Wally McArthur (trainer), Dave Bumpstead, Terry Oldfield, Norman Sykes, Joe Davis, Dave Stone, Bobby Campbell (coach). Front row: Harold Jarman, Bobby Jones, Alfie Biggs, Ian Hamilton, Brian Jenkins.

Post as to whether centre-half Joe Davis, who had recovered from an ankle injury and was fit for selection, would be picked after Bradford's performance in that position for the game against Mansfield. 'Davis' return cannot be considered automatic,' wrote Robin Perry. There was also the rivalry for the outside left position between Bradford and Brian Jenkins, if Bradford was replaced at centre-half. It was considered that Rovers' attack had invariably played better during the season when the former England forward had been on the left wing, but Tann had to consider Jenkins' form at Coventry – the best he had shown since moving to Eastville from Exeter City. In the event, Davis was recalled to the defence and Bradford selected on the left wing from where he scored the second equaliser in a 3–2 win. Rovers had not won a game in the 1963/64 season without Geoff Bradford. Whether he was playing well, indifferently or badly, his influence seemed an essential part of the form that had brought fresh hope to Eastville that winter. Bradford, now playing at outside left, fulfilled several roles in the latest extension of his distinguished career. His accurate centring and passing was used to serve Biggs and other goalscorers of the line; his adaptability allowing him to drop back and play the part of the third wing-half, either to supplement the defence or to allow the four speedier members of the attack to remain upfield. A newspaper report of the game against Gillingham in the Football League Cup that season recorded that, '. . . the left flank of Hamilton and Bradford provided much of the industry and craft.' But in cup ties he was Bradford the individual match-winner. At Bournemouth in the FA Cup first round his display when switched to centre-half after Joe Davis had been injured saved the game for Rovers. On 7 December in the second round Bradford fired Rovers into the lead at high-flying Coventry City after 6 minutes with a superb 22-yard left-foot volley that gave Bob Wesson no chance in the Sky Blues goal, and gave Rovers the confidence to despatch the Third Division leaders 2–1 from the competition.

At Eastville on the first Saturday of 1964, the goal-snatching talent that a few years earlier made Bradford the idol of the supporters again reappeared. A calmly executed volley 10 minutes from the end brought victory over Second Division Norwich City in the FA Cup. John Brown darted to the right-wing, swung over a fine centre for Bradford to score, which set up a fourth round tie against Manchester United at Old Trafford. Bradford, the last survivor of the 1952/53 championship-winning side, was also the sole survivor from the Rovers team who had caused such an upset in January 1956 when the Pirates defeated United 4–0 at Eastville. However, there was to be no repeat of the famous victory as a star-studded United side which included Bobby Charlton, Denis Law and George Best triumphed 4–1 with Law scoring a hat-trick. Geoff Bradford's final appearance for Rovers was against Reading on 21 April 1964 in the final home and penultimate match of the 1963/64 season. He had not appeared in the first team since the defeat at Manchester United and the 8,002 spectators who gathered at Eastville as Bradford took the field in his familiar no. 10 shirt were probably aware that

this would be the last they would see of their hero in Rovers colours. His final appearance of the season was his thirtieth league, FA Cup and League Cup game of the campaign, all but one in the outside left position, in which he contributed four league goals and two in the FA Cup. The final goal of his illustrious career was the winner in the 2–1 victory against Norwich City at Eastville on 4 January in the third round of the FA Cup.

The *Bristol Evening Post*'s headline for the Reading match report read, 'Sad Farewell For Bradford'. Roy Bentley made a triumphant return to his first

Geoff Bradford in an England shirt he wore during the FA tour to the West Indies in 1955 chats to team-mates Harold Jarman, Doug Hillard and Alfie Biggs.

league club – he began his career as an office boy at Eastville – when, as manager of Reading, the former Chelsea and England player watched Rovers topple to their biggest home defeat of the season. Yet for another old England player, it was a sad occasion. Bradford, back at inside left for his farewell league appearance provided nostalgic moments of cleverness, but could little more than watch as the club to which he had devoted 15 years of distinguished football service was outsmarted by an efficient, accurate and hard-working Reading side. Bradford's cameo appearance was not the triumph one would have hoped for as mid-table Rovers were defeated 5–2. With Ian Hamilton recalled to the Rovers team for the last game of the season at Crewe, Bradford contemplated his prospects, 'It is true I have no definite plans for my future. Football has been my life and I have no other trade except driving. But if the testimonial fund proves a big success I would have serious thoughts of entering a small business or taking a pub which would enable me to continue the kind of contact with the public I have enjoyed in football for 15 years. If the fund is not a success I will have to think again about finding some other kind of work,' he told an *Evening Post* reporter. However, Bradford left the Football League stage with a sense of disappointment. His playing days had been prolonged by a successful switch to full-back, after that second leg injury had deprived him of the sharpness that had made him such a feared goalscorer, and he was given reason to believe that he would be staying on to play in the reserves and to help bring on the youngsters. The let-down came when Bert Tann called him to his office and told him that, with the financial situation as it was with the club, there would not be a place for Bradford the following season after all. 'I was upset about it, but somehow felt it was not the end of my Eastville career. But then the letter came saying that my services were no longer required and that I was being given a free transfer.' Bradford had his disappointments on looking back on his career with Rovers, going as far as to say that it was 'one of the regrets of my life that I never played First Division football,' explaining that he was, 'made sharply aware of

A ticket for Bradford's Testimonial match against an International XI at Eastville.

just what I had missed' when he played in the FA Cup tie against Manchester United in front of a 56,000 crowd at Old Trafford during the 1963/64 season, his last as a professional player. 'I had appeared on First Division grounds before, but nothing quite matched up to the atmosphere of that afternoon,' he reflected. Bradford departed the Bristol football scene with a well-deserved testimonial, part of the new deal for players having changed the regulations so that clubs could now make that award for exceptional service instead of a second or third benefit.

Following his tremendous loyal service to his only professional club, Geoff became the first Rovers player to be awarded a testimonial match, on completion of fifteen years' service. It took place at Eastville Stadium on Monday 27 April 1964, when a combined Rovers and City team entertained an International XI put together by Bill Dodgin, the former Rovers player who was then chief scout with the club. Brian Clark and Bobby Williams were the City players in the Bristol side, while the International XI included Sheffield Wednesday and England goalkeeper Ron Springett, Marvin Hinton and Eddie McCreadie of Chelsea, and John Atyeo at centre forward. Robin Perry *(Bristol Evening Post)* in his press report asked the question, 'Who said Geoff Bradford was the forgotten man of Bristol football? Last night over 12,000 turned up for the testimonial paying their tribute to Bristol Rovers' greatest post-war player.'

Perry went on to say, 'Because of a toe injury, Bradford could only play for the first half – and then with the help of a pain killing injection – but his mere appearance in his old position of centre foward, however brief, was sufficient for the crowd to show their affection for this modest, lanky player who this summer completes 15 years at Eastville – years filled with fine goalscoring feats. No final figures will be ready until all the tickets are in but the gate receipts will be in the region of £2,000. A fitting send-off for a fine clubman unlikely to be retained when Rovers announce their list at the end of the week.'

The International XI took the lead after 13 minutes when Doug Hillard following a brilliant run by Chelsea winger Frank Blunstone ran the ball over his own line.

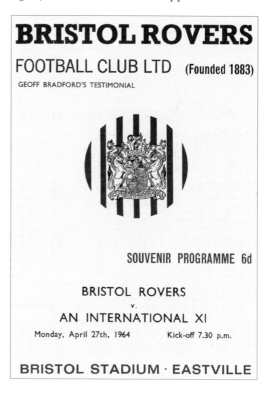

BRISTOL ROVERS

FOOTBALL CLUB LTD (Founded 1883)

GEOFF BRADFORD'S TESTIMONIAL

SOUVENIR PROGRAMME 6d

BRISTOL ROVERS
v.
AN INTERNATIONAL XI

Monday, April 27th, 1964   Kick-off 7.30 p.m.

BRISTOL STADIUM · EASTVILLE

Front cover of the programme for the testimonial game played on Monday 27 April 1964.

Ron Springett made fine full-length saves from Brian Clark and Bobby Williams who often delighted with their cleverly engineered attacks before the Bristol side equalised in the 35th minute. Bradford started the move that brought the goal by chipping a perfect pass inside to Jarman. He rolled the ball on across field to Bobby Jones, moved forward onto a return pass and drove a fierce shot wide of Springett. Suddenly a crowd with a rather dispassionate interest in the game and its snatches of superb football from the All Stars warmed to the Bristol side. The match at once had atmosphere. A roar of appreciation greeted Jones' great run in from the left and the shot that crashed against the far post and another spectacular Springett save from Clark's powerful drive. But 2 minutes from half time Bryan Douglas, of Blackburn Rovers, always a fascinating mixture of clever footwork and tantalising bursts of acceleration, put the International XI ahead again from Alan Skirton's pulled back centre. It was a low drive and the bounce of it deceived Bernard Hall who let the ball over his shoulder.

With Geoff's disappearance at half time, replaced by Alfie Biggs, the pressure was really turned on by the guests when John Atyeo galloped 60 yards to collect a delayed Douglas through-pass and drive it past Hall and 2 minutes later it was 4–1 as Arsenal's Skirton, the towering Bath-born winger, outjumped the defence to nod in Douglas's fine centre from the right. The game remained eventful as Springett saved well from Jones and Mabbutt. Atyeo presented with a completely unguarded goal side-footed the ball wide but minutes later it was only Hall's brilliance that prevented a fierce rising drive from the centre forward from sneaking under the bar. 'We tried to get a top First Division team down,' said Bradford after the game, 'but they were all tied up in various competitions or had tour commitments. There was a large crowd, but by the time I had paid all the match expenses and £25 appearance money to each player in the All Stars team there was not a great deal left. The Supporters' Club stepped in with a generous donation, and in the end I cleared £1,500. I didn't realise it was to be soccer's parting gift.'

In the match programme, Pat Kavanagh, reporter for the *Bristol Evening World*, wrote that 'Geoff's ice-cold scheming and the natural ability he possesses have always been hidden beneath a calm, unassuming manner – this facet of his character has endeared him to me. Geoff has been one of Britain's post-war greats,' remarking that, 'he had never seen Bradford petulant, let alone lose his temper.' John Coe, *Bristol Evening Post* journalist, who covered Rovers' home matches from 1938 to 1961 also made a moving tribute in the programme stating Bradford was 'the greatest player ever to have played for Bristol Rovers' in the 40 years he had been watching soccer at Eastville. 'He has superb ball-control, accurate passing, an unerring sense of timing, a polished precision stemming from natural ability and intelligent anticipation, a powerful well directed shot and physical fitness. He has shown personal courage in the face of cruel and gross injuries which would have ended long since the career of a lesser person. When I think of Bradford I recall a skilled craftsman, a craftsman of an innate gentle nature, whose loyalty to the game, his club and his team-mates make some of the money-grabbing miscreants up and down the country look the shabby characters they are. When I think of his red-letter days I recall an evening game at Eastville when he scored three goals against Liverpool. It was the kind of art which conceals art,' adding further, 'And when I think of the club he has adorned I tell myself that had it been a more glamorous organisation, Bradford would have played for England more often than he did.'

Bradford stands alone as Bristol Rovers' greatest player, scorer of eleven hat-tricks (ending with all four goals against Rotherham on 14 March 1959) in a league haul that puts him more than 60 ahead of the club's next highest aggregate scorer, Alfie Biggs. Yet, he admitted that he was 'a lazy inside forward', and because of that there were times when he used get 'some stick', as he put it from some of his team-mates, but Geoff Fox used to say: 'As long as he keeps putting the ball in the net leave him alone. When he stops scoring then you can get on at him.' It appears that Jackie Pitt gave him his nickname of 'RIP'. Some believed it was an abbreviation for Rest in Peace, while others thought it referred to Rip Van Winkle, a character who slept for twenty years in a short story by the American author Washington Irving. Whichever explanation is true it was not a reflection of his play on the field, but of his ability to rest and sleep even in the last hour before a game. 'As time went on,' recalled Bradford, 'and the team changed and the game itself began to make more demands, I had to work much harder than I did in those early days. In fact, I did far more work after switching to centre foward than I ever did as an inside forward.'

Basil Easterbrook, a regular contributor to *Charles Buchan's Football Monthly* magazine had this to say about Rovers' finest player following his retirement.

> Geoff Bradford had two great assets which lifted him above the ruck – his intuition which permitted him to move in and out of position at the right time and his fearlessness which let him beat the tackle by that vital spilt second. Bradford like all the really fine players was good without the ball and able to put up a show in almost any position, but it will be as a marksman and leader that he will be best remembered. Never a showy player, and a careful conserver of energy, Geoff Bradford even had his critics among Rovers supporters for not grafting at times. These people forgot his amazing goal flair which made him the greatest match-winner ever to wear the blue-and-white quarters of Bristol Rovers.

9

LIFE AFTER FOOTBALL

Within a week of his testimonial match and facing an uncertain future, Bradford made a tentative enquiry as to whether, if necessary, Bristol Rovers Supporters' Club would advance the money to help him obtain a public house pending receipt from his testimonial fund. The committee agreed that there was no reason why the cash should not be handed over fairly soon and decided to await developments. Geoff extended an invitation to supporters' club committee members to a meal on Friday 29 May and it was agreed by the committee that at the function a cheque as a contribution to his testimonial fund would be presented to him. It transpired that the net amount payable to Bradford from the football club was £1,416 7s 1d and it was unanimously agreed to make a donation of £600 to the testimonial fund. At the beginning of June he approached the chairman of the supporters' club, Eric Godfrey, regarding the possibility of a loan of £3,000 to enable him to obtain a public house, but it was felt that this was too large a sum for the committee to sanction and that the matter would have to be submitted to the AGM. But there the matter seems to have rested. Following his testimonial match, Bradford at the age of 36, after temporarily joining the supporters' club lottery staff, finished completely with football not having any desire to coach or play at amateur level. But he still of course kept a close eye on his beloved Bristol Rovers' progress and results, watching as many matches as he could get to. His personal friendship with Bristol City legend John Atyeo continued long after both men retired from the professional game. They both had a great respect for each other and both men met every week during the football season to predict draws for the Spastics' Football Pools organisation, a registered charity based in Stokes Croft, Bristol, mulling over the fixtures while on a small panel of experts. Despite their great on field rivalry, with Atyeo challenging Bradford's right to be seen as the city's footballing top dog, the two Bristol footballing kings of the period were great friends. The 1950s were a thrilling time for Bristol football, with both teams pushing for the top division, but the stark and surprising fact was that right through the 1950s City were consistently second-best to their Eastville rivals in terms of league position. When Fred Ford was appointed as City's manager in July 1960 there was great concern at first among City supporters who did not know what to make of the signing of Rovers' coach as their team's boss, but to the players he was just another football man to be judged on his own merits, and they soon decided he had plenty of these. Atyeo recalled, 'When Fred Ford came, I remember talking to Geoff Bradford about him, and he told me:

You can't go wrong now. He's the best man you can possibly have for the job.' Atyeo was one of a number of friends in the football world who Geoff kept in contact with, the two of them often grumbling about the wages being paid to the modern nonentities, but would always end with the mutually reassuring: 'I'm glad we were playing then, rather than now.' Towards the end of his life Bradford reminisced about his great friend and the period they both played in, 'I have great memories of the 1950s. Both the Bristol clubs had great sides in those years and produced great attacking football. It was a pleasure to play in those years and it must have been a great pleasure for the fans to watch. I am a very good friend of John Atyeo and we often talk of those great days. In our day it was great football and no money. I feel sorry for the fans who have to pay so much money to watch it,' he recalled in 1992.

It is fair to say that after Geoff finished playing for Rovers he was upset by his treatment by the club after fifteen years' exemplary service. Having finished playing for the club he used to visit the dressing rooms early before matches to chat to the players, but Rovers stopped him from doing this and then the club wanted to charge him for going to watch games. As a result he never went back to Eastville Stadium, but was nonetheless still intensely interested in his beloved Rovers' results and was devastated when the club moved from its historic home to Bath in 1986.

As a consequence of his playing days being over, in about 1966, the Bradford family had to vacate the Rovers-owned house they inhabited in Dormer Road, which was subsequently

Geoff with wife Betty and their three daughters Nichola, Lesley and Lynn pictured in 1964.

occupied by Rovers' defender Terry Oldfield and his wife. They were rehoused by Bristol City Council to 638 Portway, near what was later the Robin Cousins Sports Centre. The house has since been demolished and replaced by one of the concrete pillars supporting the M5 bridge over the River Avon. While living there Geoff worked at nearby Avonmouth Docks. From Shirehampton, Geoff and Betty took over as mine hosts at the Golden Lion pub in Fishponds Road which Geoff enjoyed running, partly because of the male company, which in some ways was reminiscent of the times spent with his playing colleagues, and also the activities that took place in the pub, such as darts and crib, a game that he was particularly good at. He had learned and played many card games on his numerous long away trips with Rovers and often played card games with his family, but because of the difficulty of being able to take time off from running the pub, Geoff and Betty decided to get out of the licensed trade and moved to Lawrence Weston, living at 14 Shortlands Road. Geoff then joined Shell Mex & BP Ltd based at Avonmouth as a lorry driver delivering fuel oil and at times petrol in a small lorry that he referred to as a 'Piss Pot', having been recommended to the company by one of his relatives who already worked for the firm. Geoff had learnt to drive while serving in the army and the tanker driving job required him to work shifts and on occasions necessitated working throughout the night. Working for Shell Mex for over 25 years entitled Geoff to a pension from the company following his retirement.

In November 1966, Bradford played in a charity football match for TWW All Stars, which included his old friend John Atyeo, former Rovers team-mates Dai Ward and Geoff Fox plus local television presenter Bruce Hockin, a good friend of Geoff, who played in goal for

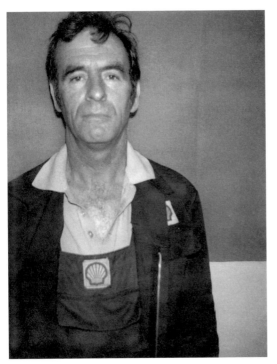

the 'Show Biz' team against the Legion Stars. The game was organised by the Royal British Legion to raise funds for the families of the 116 children and 28 adults who were killed when a colliery spoil heap in the coalmining village of Aberfan, near Merthyr Tydfil, collapsed on 21 October, destroying a school and numerous homes.

The Bradfords' next home was at 45 Oakdale Road in Downend, a location close to Cleeve Hill Tennis Club. At the age of 47 after ten years of inactivity he returned to playing lawn tennis at the club near his home on the outskirts of Bristol. During his playing days in the

On his retirement from football Geoff spent over twenty-five years working as a petrol/oil tanker driver for Shell Mex at Avonmouth in Bristol.

football close season, Geoff regularly played tennis at the Bristol Civil Service Club in Filton Avenue, Horfield, with Rovers' manager Bert Tann, coach Fred Ford and team-mates Peter Hooper and Howard Radford, who were all keen opponents. He was good enough to play league tennis, representing the club's second team remarking that it was a good standard but he was beyond the first team which included many county players. A keen sportsman with ability in many fields, Geoff enjoyed playing a variety of sports beside football throughout his life. He played cricket for Fishponds Royal British Legion and acted as an umpire, as well as being a regular member of a Rovers team that played friendlies against local cricket sides, took part in athletics, regularly played lawn tennis and as a young boy boxed. Angling was a particularly favourite pastime and as a keen fisherman he would always buy a fishing licence wherever he happened to be on holiday, spending many happy hours with his rod and reel. Locally he was a member of the Silver Dace Angling Association, a fishing club based at St Ambrose church hall in Whitehall who, among other places, fished on the River Avon near the Chequers pub in Hanham and 'Jack White's' by the Lock Keeper pub in Keynsham. Geoff's daughter Lynn vividly remembers family fishing trips to Bradford-on-Avon with, on cold frosty mornings, the smell of her mum's bacon and burgers wafting downstream tantalising the tastebuds of other anglers, while her father 'would have to put the maggots on the hooks as we were too squeamish!'

Once when the Bradford family were on holiday in Devon, Geoff proved to be one of the heroes who helped to save a young man's life. He had fallen into a fast-flowing river and was in danger of being swept out to sea. Despite being unable to swim himself Geoff formed part of the human chain that stretched across the river and managed to stop the man as he surged down the river. Perhaps non-swimmer Geoff felt safe in venturing into the water as his birth had been 'en caul', a term used to describe a child born inside of the entire amniotic sac, which balloons out at birth, with the child remaining inside of the unbroken or partially broken membrane. A legend developed suggesting that possession of a baby's caul would give its bearer good luck and protect that person from death by drowning. Cauls were therefore highly prized by sailors. Geoff kept his caul wrapped in paper in his wallet throughout his life and took it with him everywhere he went. Geoff had a very close relationship with his brother Don, who died of a heart attack in 1982 at the age of 61. Donald had suffered from angina, as had Geoff.

Geoff was a great help domestically, particularly after wife Betty injured her back. He would do the housework and prepare food, his *pièce de résistance* being home-made mushroom soup. Betty worked as a nurse in a children's ward at Purdown Hospital and on one occasion, being the kind and caring person that she was, tried to pick up a child who had fallen on the floor, but in attempting to do so severely damaged her back, being told subsequently that she may never walk again. Thankfully this was not the case, but it did curtail her ability to work.

Geoff owned a knitting machine and would make jumpers for his daughters when the family were living in Dormer Road, and also did sewing and tapestry. He watched a lot of televised football matches after he retired from the game, and particularly liked watching John Wayne films when broadcast on the television. Geoff enjoying listening to music and was given an electronic organ as a present which he often played, and spent many hours

Don Bradford, left, Geoff's older brother, was best man at Geoff's wedding in 1951.

Rovers celebrated their centenary in 1983 with a friendly match against Newcastle United at Eastville. Former players were invited as special guests. Left to right: Bryan Bush, Bill Roost, Bert Hoyle, Josser Watling, Geoff Bradford, Ray Warren and Geoff Fox are acknowledged by the crowd.

avidly doing jigsaw puzzles. He also had somewhat of a mischievous side to his character as demonstrated in an incident recalled by his daughters when he attended a party at a playing colleague's house. His Rovers team-mate had recently bought a new fridge and was very proud of his latest acquisition, until Geoff decided to paint the pristine appliance bright red. Geoff took great pleasure in regularly helping daughter Lynn organise Bishopston Rugby Club's annual dinner, preparing the food and laying places at tables for up to 200 guests. He loved tending his garden and working in the greenhouse where he grew seedlings for his family, roses and fuchsias being his favourite flowers. Described by his daughters as 'a well-loved real family man' he enjoyed spending time with his seven grandchildren, in some ways making up for the time that he had been unable to spend with his own daughters owing to the amount of time he was away from home as a professional footballer.

On 6 December 1983 Bradford was well received by Bristol Rovers fans, many of whom never saw him play, as he and many of his former team-mates including Bert Hoyle, Geoff Fox, Jackie Pitt, Ray Warren, Peter Sampson, George Petherbridge and Alfie Biggs were introduced to the crowd at Eastville before Rovers celebrated their centenary by playing a match against Newcastle United.

Rovers' groundsman and stalwart player Jackie Pitt enjoyed a well-earned testimonial match in 1988 against FA Cup holders Wimbledon. Many of Pitt's former team-mates were invited to the match at Twerton Park. Left to right: Doug Hillard, Peter Sampson, George Petherbridge, Alfie Biggs, Bill Roost, Harry Liley, Jackie Pitt with the FA Cup, Geoff Bradford, Bryan Bush.

On 13 August 1988 Geoff, as a guest of Rovers – with some of his former team-mates – attended Jackie Pitt's testimonial match at Twerton Park. Bobby Gould's FA Cup winners Wimbledon played Gerry Francis' exiled Rovers side.

Geoff and Betty's final residence was at 89 Avonsmere Residential Park, Filton, where they made their home from the 1980s for the final years of his life before his health deteriorated. Prior to moving to Avonsmere, Geoff and Betty went to London to have a chalet built to their own specifications prior to delivery to the Filton site. They named their home Yer Tis. One visitor to their north Bristol home was life-long Rovers fan, Philip Turner, who during the school holidays in the 1950s had on many occasions waited with his autograph scrapbooks for Rovers players to arrive for training, to repeatedly ask the question, 'Would you sign please, Mr Bradford?' And thirty years later was looking for one more signature. Philip's recollection of the visit to his hero's home is indicative of the high esteem that Bradford was held in by the fans, both for his playing ability and for the gentleman he was, and is a fitting fan tribute of Rovers' hat-trick hero. Having bought two copies of the book *Bristol Rovers – A Complete Record 1883–1987* in December 1987, Phil attempted to contact his boyhood idol to obtain his autograph once more:

> I telephoned the number that I had found in the telephone directory and asked the lady who answered, 'Would I be on the right number for Mr Geoff Bradford, who used to play for Bristol Rovers?' I was already answering her in my mind with a thank you, sorry to trouble you, but I received the unexpected reply of, 'Yes you would.'

This immediately sent the middle-aged, married man with children into stutter mode as he nervously started to ask:

> 'Oh, yes, well I've um bought this book . . .' 'Would you like to speak to him?' the lady responded, putting me out of my awkwardness, and then I went into shock mode. I think the phone at my end started to shake slightly in my hand as I answered politely, 'Yes, please', and then waited a few seconds wondering how one should address one's hero. The calm assured voice that next greeted me made me relax and feel a lot more comfortable very quickly, as I started to explain that I had bought two Rovers books, one for myself and the second to give as a Christmas present to my best friend Barry Dyte, and wondered if Geoff would sign the inside cover of each. Without hesitation I was invited to visit Geoff's home with the books for signing and we agreed a convenient time and day, and then all I had to do was look forward to meeting the great man. A few days later, at the appointed time, I was welcomed into the home of Geoff Bradford by the lady who I had spoken to on the telephone, who was obviously Mrs Bradford. I received a warm handshake from Geoff and, as Mrs Bradford retired to prepare the tea she had offered, our conversation quickly turned to football, blue-and-white quarters, goals scored, etc, and as we reminisced I was in awe at the way this warm-hearted, modest man talked about games and events and made them appear they happened the previous week. There were reminders of Rovers' golden days written in the book that came back to Geoff as he keenly checked records

and reports and commented accordingly, as I sat mesmerised. Geoff quickly made me feel like an old friend who he had known for years as I absorbed the details behind the many things that had occurred on the pitch. I well remember the fact that my favourite player was so modest as he recalled actions and events that had caused thirty thousand plus crowds to cheer and shout with such passion and pleasure. He listened intently to my answer to his question asking if I had played football. I was pleased to tell him I had worn the no. 9 shirt many times and scored fifty-eight goals in the 1965/66 season although I hastened to point out I was talking a local park league, but I will treasure the memory of Geoff Bradford, the world famous footballer, congratulating me and saying I must have had the knack as well. Those words from, in my opinion, the greatest player to wear a Rovers shirt were words that dreams are made of. After about an hour Geoff asked if he should sign the books which he duly did providing his autograph and a personalised message for each of the volumes' recipients. A gentleman and gentle man, and in all my conversations about Bristol Rovers and Geoff Bradford I have never met anyone who has said anything remotely unpleasant about this lovely man and only all the right adjectives come to mind by way of reference to this special footballer and man. Geoff's family and friends, can be rightly, very proud of him as are the people who were associated with him, and that naturally makes him one of the top sporting personalities of Bristol . . . EVER.

While living at Filton Geoff kindly wrote the foreword for the Mike Jay and Stephen Byrne's book, *Pirates in Profile: A Who's Who of Bristol Rovers Players 1920–1994*, which was published in 1994. His last public appearance was ironically at Ashton Gate where he represented Rovers in a parade of the stars of yesteryear, honouring his old friend and rival John Atyeo, at the official opening on Saturday 8 October 1994 of the newly built Carling Atyeo Stand. Officially opened by Sir Bert Millichip, Chairman of the Football Association, before a home game with Millwall, also celebrating the opening were twenty-two City 'old boys'.

Geoff signs a copy of Mike Jay's book *Bristol Rovers – A Complete Record 1883–1987*, for long-time Rovers fan Philip Turner, December 1987.

Manager Bert Tann a highly respected coach and tactician who moulded Rovers into a formidable team throughout the 1950s.

Geoff Bradford passed peacefully away on 30 December 1994 at the age of 67, after a fight against cancer. His wife Betty died on Boxing Day 2005 aged 75. Geoff's funeral service was held at 3.15 p.m. at St John the Baptist's Church, Frenchay, just off the common in that village on the northern outskirts of Bristol where he and his family had lived some 50 years before. Around 150 packed into the little church for the service, which ended with the emotional singing of Rovers' anthem 'Goodnight Irene'. Former team-mates at the funeral included Paddy Hale, Bobby Jones, Harold Jarman, Ray Mabbutt, Alfie Biggs and George Petherbridge. Bristol Rovers mourners were led by chairman Dennis Dunford and manager John Ward, and the team's leading goalscorer at the time Marcus Stewart was joined by captain Andy Tilson and goalkeeper Brian Parkin. Alan Williams, the former Bristol City centre-half who marked Bradford in many games between the rivals, stayed outside the packed church, saying: 'I don't want to go in, but I felt I just had to be here because I had great respect for Geoff.' Mrs Marina Dolman, widow of former Bristol City Chairman Harry Dolman said 'My husband always had a sneaking regard for Geoff Bradford.' Rector Roger Thomas recalled being at Eastville to see Bradford score on many occasions. He told the congregation, 'Geoff was my boyhood idol. I remember seeing him score many great goals, including a hat-trick against Liverpool. He is part of the history of Bristol's football and when Rovers build their new stadium I hope they name a stand after him. Geoff said he wanted his funeral here to be near his manager Bert Tann, who is buried in our cemetery.'

His old boss, who had lived nearby in a Cotswold stone house in Grange Park, died on 12 July 1972 aged 58 years and is buried in the church graveyard. Geoff's funeral service was followed by cremation at Westerleigh cemetery in South Gloucestershire.

There can be no more eloquent or fitting tribute to Bristol Rovers' finest player than the one given by the club's secretary John Gummow on the night of Thursday 8 May 1959 when Geoff Bradford became the first recipient of the Harry Bamford Memorial Trophy.

Geoff has graced the game here in Bristol with great distinction, and in a long and eventful career has given pleasure to many thousands of people both in his native city and throughout Great Britain and abroad. Twice his courage has triumphed over the adversity of the severest injuries. Not once in all the games in which he has played in the colours of Bristol Rovers has a referee ever had occasion to question his conduct. Off the field of play, it would be difficult indeed to imagine anyone so unassuming and so modest of his own achievements. Like his great friend, Harry Bamford, there was nothing unkind in his personality and he will be remembered with affection by generations of Bristolians, not only for the pleasure he has given them with so much skill, but also by the manner in which he has always played the game, thus emphasising the fact that a game does not cease to be a game because a man is paid to play it.

OBITUARY

Geoffrey Reginald William Bradford, footballer: born Bristol 18 July 1927; played for Bristol Rovers 1949–64; capped once for England 1955; died Bristol 30 December 1994. Football in general, and Bristol Rovers in particular, could do with more men like Geoff Bradford. He was the most prolific goal-scorer in that homely club's history; he remains the only 'Pirate' to win a full England cap; and, were it possible to hold a cross-generation poll of fans to determine the finest player ever to wear Rovers' distinctive blue-and-white quarters, the odds would be heavily in favour of the gentle, acutely unassuming Bristolian coming out on top. When Bradford was in his bountiful 1950s prime, he was accorded a sporting celebrity in the West Country exceeded only by that of his close friend and rival the late John Atyeo of Bristol City; meanwhile at grounds around the country, he was often the only Rovers player of whom supporters had heard. The acclaim, however, never turned his head, and when the two men were together at a function, invariably Bradford would ask the more outgoing (though also modest) Atyeo to deal with the demands of press and public. Bradford's impressive record – 262 goals in 512 senior outings – owed much to a sharp-edged technical talent which contrasted vividly with his unthrusting personality. He was as clean, accurate and powerful a striker of the ball with either foot as could be found outside the game's top division (in which, sadly, he never played), his touch was subtle and certain, his timing in the air was intuitive. To these gifts were added a natural resilience which saw him return in triumph from two fearful leg injuries which might have put him out of football for good. His critics called him lazy, but Bradford, known as 'Rip' to team-mates because of his knack for sleeping before a match, could justifiably refer them to his goal tally. His England chance came in October 1955, against Denmark in Copenhagen, when he scored once and made another for Tom Finney in a 5–1 victory. It seemed enough to warrant a second call but this never arrived and Bradford returned uncomplainingly to bread-and-butter duty with Rovers, who had plucked him from local amateur ranks in 1949 and who remained his only professional club. The highlight of Bradford's 15 years at Eastville – the much-loved home of the Pirates until a controversial move to Bath in 1986 – came in 1952/53 when his club record of 33 goals did much to secure the Division III (South) Championship. Had his peak years not coincided with football's maximum-wage restriction, it is reasonable to suppose that such a talent would have moved on to more lucrative fields, but all who revelled in his exploits as a Rover would find it hard to imagine their faithful spearhead in the colours of another club. After his retirement in 1964, Bradford became a petrol tanker driver, continuing to live quietly in the city of his birth.

Ivan Ponting, *The Independent*

10

STATISTICS AND RECORDS

When Geoff Bradford made his league debut for Bristol Rovers on 24 September 1949 at Crystal Palace he became the 296th player to make their debut for the club since they were elected to the Football League in 1920. Only Stuart Taylor 546, from a later era (1965–80) Harry Bamford 486 and Jackie Pitt 467, exceeded Geoff Bradford's 461 league appearances. Five of his team-mates remarkably made over 400 appearances, namely George Petherbridge 457, Ray Warren 450, Harold Jarman 440, Alfie Biggs 424 and Bobby Jones 421. Of course Geoff had two long periods out of the game with serious injury, almost six months during 1953/54 and three months during 1955/56, so had he not sustained these long-term injuries his appearances and goals tally would have been even more. By the time of his final league appearance on 21 April 1964 a further 178 new debutants had played for the club, some 375 players since election to the Football League in 1920. Geoff's league career spanned 14 years 210 days.

Senior Appearances and Goals

Season	League		FA Cup		Glos Cup		League Cup		Totals	
	apps	goals	apps	goals	apps	goals	apps	goals	apps	goals
1949/50	18	3	0	0	1	0	n/a		19	3
1950/51	36	15	11	3	1	0	n/a		48	18
1951/52	45	26	4	3	1	0	n/a		50	29
1952/53	45	33	4	1	1	0	n/a		50	34
1953/54	18	21	0	0	0	0	n/a		18	21
1954/55	39	26	2	1	1	0	n/a		42	27
1955/56	26	25	3	1	0	0	n/a		29	26
1956/57	25	11	2	2	1	1	n/a		28	14
1957/58	33	20	5	2	1	1	n/a		39	23
1958/59	33	20	1	0	1	0	n/a		35	20
1959/60	30	12	0	0	1	0	n/a		31	12
1960/61	32	12	0	0	1	0	2	1	35	13
1961/62	39	12	2	0	1	0	3	2	45	14
1962/63	21	2	1	0	1	0	2	0	25	2
1963/64	21	4	4	2	0	0	5	0	30	6
Totals	461	242	39	15	12	2	12	3	524	262

Easily Bristol Rovers' record aggregate scorer, with a staggering 242 goals in league football, Bradford achieved a ratio of a goal every two games over fifteen seasons. Bradford also made over 70 appearances for Bristol Rovers reserves scoring over 50 goals and more than 10 appearances for the club in the Western League, scoring 9 goals.

Geoff Bradford's medal collection. Top row, left to right: the coveted Football League Champions Division Three (Southern Section), the Football League vs League of Ireland, Dublin 1954. Middle row: Gloucestershire FA Senior Professional Cup Winners medals v Bristol City 1948/49, 1954/55, 1962/63. Bottom row: Trinidad FA Commemorative Medal 1955, Curaçao FA badge 1955, Trinidad FA badge 1955, FA tour to the West Indies 1955.

TEN OUTFIELD POSITIONS

Besides being a potent goalscorer during his long and successful career, Geoff remarkably appeared in nine outfield positions for the Bristol Rovers first team, demonstrating his worth as a utility player as well: Right full-back 32; left full-back 1; centre-half 4; left half-back 1; outside right 3; inside right 112; centre forward 217; inside left 121 and outside left 33. Rovers' club records show that he also made at least two appearances at right half-back for Rovers' Western League side in a 5–3 defeat against Bath City Reserves on 17 November 1962 and in his final season, for the reserves when they defeated Ipswich Town 4–1 at Eastville on 29 February 1964.

GOALS RECORD

First league goal   4 March 1950, Walsall, lost 1–3 at Fellows Park
Last league goal   14 December 1963, Bristol City, won 4–0 at Eastville
Last goal   4 January 1964, Norwich City (FA Cup), won 2–1 at Eastville

Bradford and centre forward Alfie Biggs who spent fifteen seasons in two spells with the club (1953–61 and 1962–8), both scored against 55 different clubs in the league while winger Harold Jarman (1959–71) scored against 53 different clubs in his career which spanned fourteen seasons.

HAT-TRICKS

Bradford scored 11 Football League hat-tricks during his 15-year career, against: Torquay United, Newport County, Fulham, Brentford, Notts County, Luton Town, Stoke City, Derby County, Liverpool, Hull City and Rotherham United (4 goals). Five of those trebles came in 1953/54, Rovers' first season in Division Two. He also scored four hat-tricks in FA representative games against the RAF in 1953, a Jamaican XI (twice), and Trinidad on the 1955 tour of the West Indies.

FA CUP RECORDS

Rovers' top FA Cup appearance maker of all time is George Petherbridge (40 games), followed by Geoff Bradford (39) and Stuart Taylor (38). Vic Lambden scored 16 FA Cup goals for the club, followed by Bradford (15) and Alfie Biggs (13) – Jack Jones scored 18, when Rovers were a Southern League Club though many of these games were in cup qualifiers, so not always considered for records of this type. Bradford's first FA Cup goal was on 5 December 1950 at Cardiff City in a replay against Llanelly when he scored in a

3–1 extra time win, with his final cup goal being over 13 years later on 4 January 1964 in a 2–1 victory over Norwich City at Eastville.

FOOTBALL LEAGUE CUP RECORDS

Geoff made 12 appearances in the competition which was introduced in the 1960/61 season specifically as a midweek floodlit tournament, and he played and scored in the very first League Cup tie on 26 September 1960 when Rovers defeated Fulham 2–1 at Eastville in front of over 20,000 fans. He scored 3 League Cup goals, all at Eastville, against Fulham in the inaugural year, and Hartlepool and Blackburn Rovers in 1961/62.

ENGLAND RECORD

When Geoff made his solitary full international appearance for England in the 5–1 victory over Denmark at Idrætsparken, Copenhagen, on 2 October 1955, he had scored 135 goals in 210 league matches for Bristol Rovers. He was 28 years and 76 days old when making his international debut.

ENGLAND

Ronald Baynham
1 Luton Town

Jeffrey Hall
2 Birmingham City

Roger Byrne
3 Manchester United

William McGarry
4 Huddersfield Town

William Wright
5 Wolverhamton Wanderers

James Dickinson
6 Portsmouth

Jack Milburn
7 Newcastle U.

Donald Revie
8 Manchester C.

Nathanial Lofthouse
9 Bolton Wanderers

Geoffrey Bradford
10 Bristol Rovers

Thomas Finney
11 Preston North End

Poul Pedersen
11 AIA

Knud Lundberg
10 AB

Ove Andersen
9 Brønshøj

Jørgen Jacobsen
8 B. 93

Jørgen Hansen
7 Næstved

Jørgen Olesen
6 AGF

Chr Brøgger
5 AB

Erik Jensen
4 AB

Verner Nielsen
3 AB

Poul Andersen
2 SIF

Per Henriksen
1 Frem

Dommer: Giorgio Bernardini, Bologna
Linievogtere: Eric Johansson (Helsingborg) og Eric Storck (Malmø)

DANMARK

Geoff Bradford (1927 – 1994)
Bristol Rovers and England
The shirt and cap proudly worn by Geoff Bradford
in the England game against Denmark
on October 2, 1955

Also available from The History Press

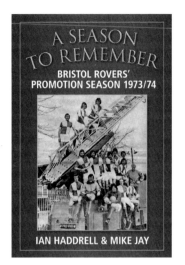

A Season to Remember: Bristol Rovers' Promotion Season 1973/74

9780752458328

In the 1973/74 season, Bristol Rovers clinched promotion to the old 'Second Division' in one of the club's most memorable campaigns. Thanks largely to the prolific goalscoring partnership between Bruce Bannister and Alan Warboys, dubbed 'Smash and Grab' by the national press, and a superb team spirit, manager Don Megson's side went unbeaten for thirty-two games, setting a new club record. This is the story of that remarkable season, featuring many previously unpublished photographs, statistics and reports of every match.

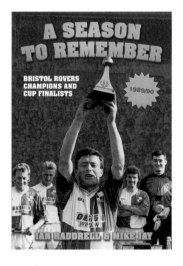

A Season to Remember: Bristol Rovers Champions and Cup Finalists 1989/90

97807524 64480

In the 1989/90 season, Bristol Rovers clinched promotion to the old 'Second Division', thanks largely to the tremendous team spirit of a side exiled in Bath, away from its traditional Bristol home. The 'Ragbag Rovers', as they became known, set an outstanding club record, remaining undefeated in 41 matches throughout the season, the highlight of which was a 3–0 victory against local rivals Bristol City in the penultimate game of the season. This remarkable time is remembered through many previously unpublished photographs, statistics and reports from every match and interviews with the players involved.

Visit our website and discover thousands of other History Press books.
www.thehistorypress.co.uk